CHARACTER BUILDING FOR FAMILIES

Volume 1

by Lee Ann Rubsam

Full Gospel Family Publications
Appleton, Wisconsin

... In lowliness of mind let each esteem other better than themselves. Look not every man on his own things, but every man also on the things of others. -- Philippians 2:3, 4

Copyright 1994, 2004, 2012 (3rd Edition) by Lee Ann Rubsam

All rights reserved. No part of this book shall be in any way reproduced without the express permission of the author.

Printed in the United States of America.

Other Publications by Lee Ann Rubsam:

River Life: Entering into the Character of Jesus
Hotline to Heaven: Hearing the Voice of God
Character Building for Families, Volume 2
House of Prayer ~ House of Power
Encouragement from God's Word
How to Pray and Read the Bible
The Intercessor's Companion
The Beginning Intercessor
The Intercessor Manual
God's Word on Healing
The Names of God

Full Gospel Family Publications
419 East Taft Avenue
Appleton, Wisconsin 54915
FullGospelFamily.com
(920) 734-6693

CHARACTER BUILDING FOR FAMILIES
VOLUME 1

TABLE OF CONTENTS

How to Use This Manual i

An Introduction to Character Building for Parents and Children 1

Obedience 2

Orderliness 9

Diligence 14

Loyalty 23

Deference 36

Cheerfulness (Joy) 41

Gentleness (Kindness) 47

Contentment 54

Gratitude 64

Truthfulness 72

Servanthood 83

Hospitality 96

HOW TO USE THIS MANUAL

Character Building for Families is a topical unit study of Christian character traits we should all wish to develop in order to be more like Jesus. It is written in outline form for easy reading.

Character Building for Families is designed to be led by one or both parents in a family devotions setting or as part of a home school curriculum. It can be used with just about any age range from five years and older, with as few or as many children as your family holds. (I used this set of studies with our children starting at about six years old, through the elementary years.)

Each unit study is broken down into daily topics. Lesson time varies, with some lessons taking twenty minutes to complete, some a little less time, some a little more. The manual is not set up on a weekly basis, so if you miss a day or two, simply continue on where you left off, free of guilt and pressure to catch up.

The only resource you will need for the studies, beyond this manual, is your Bible. (Each reading child should also have his own Bible available.) Any Bible translation will work nicely; however, the studies are designed with the King James Version in mind, so the KJV will work best. If not using King James, you may want to have one handy for quick reference, for the occasional times when the discussion questions may not seem to fit with the Bible passage you are reading. (This will be rare.)

Comments in the outlines which have direct quotation marks around them are intended to be what the parent would say to the children. I have used the question and answer discussion method as much as possible to get the children to participate and learn through their own discoveries of what God's Word says, rather than feeding them answers through lecturing.

Our family found that the simplest way for us to memorize the Bible verses was simply to read them aloud five times daily while doing the lessons. In very little time, long before a unit was done, our children could recite the verses by heart – but I took much longer.

When we did the studies in our home, sometimes we read the passages aloud, taking turns, and sometimes I directed everyone to read silently before we discussed the verses. It's good to get the children involved in the reading if they are able, rather than reading everything to them.

It is important to review the lessons from time to time, as there is so much to take in. This could be done by reviewing each unit in summary when it has been completed, before going on to the next unit; reviewing after two or three units have been completed; or finishing the entire manual and then repeating the units at a later date. Some units will be more useful than others to your family, and these should be repeated more often.

It is also not necessary to do the unit studies in the order they appear in this book. This was the order in which God laid them on my heart for my family; it may not be the order He wants you to follow at all. Pray for guidance and wisdom!

I would like to encourage parents to frequently add examples from your own experience. Tell your children how God taught you about this or that truth. Share your failures, as well as your successes. It will humble you, and make the lessons "stick" for your children. Also emphasize that you are all learning together as a family. Mom and Dad will be growing in these character traits along with the children.

God bless and enrich you as you search His Word together as a family.

AN INTRODUCTION TO CHARACTER BUILDING
FOR PARENTS AND CHILDREN

I. "We're going to be studying character traits together as a family so that we can grow into the image (likeness) of Jesus. These character traits go hand-in-hand with the fruit of the Spirit, which are found in the Bible, in Galatians 5:22,23."
    (Read Galatians 5:22,23 aloud together and discuss any words not understood by the children.)

II. "We'll be talking about one character trait at a time. We might take two weeks, or much more than two weeks for each one -- depending on how much time it takes to thoroughly cover our topic."

III. "What is a character trait?" (Allow responses.)
    A. "Good character traits are **qualities we possess** that reflect Jesus' qualities."
    B. "Our character traits will be noticed by others whether they are good character traits or bad ones. We want good ones to show so that we are good witnesses for Jesus."
    C. Read Matthew 5:16 together, discuss in light of the above comments, and recite together to begin memorization.

IV. "We will be:
    A. Looking up and studying Scripture verses to go with each character trait we are studying,
    B. Thinking about where we need improvement, and
    C. Praying for God's help in changing the way we think, speak, and act."

V. "We don't want to just know **about** good character traits; we want these traits to be blossoming in our lives." (Read James 1:22 and discuss.)

VI. "You and Mom and Dad will be learning and growing together. Mom and Dad are expecting Jesus to change us just like He will be changing you."

VII. Review what has been said by having children summarize the material in their own words. Then briefly go over any points they have missed.

VIII. Review and recite the three Scripture verses already discussed:
    A. Galatians 5:22,23 (fruit of the Spirit are some character traits)
    B. Matthew 5:16 (why have good character traits)
    C. James 1:22 (applying to our lives)

OBEDIENCE

DAY 1

I. "The first character trait we'll be studying is OBEDIENCE."
   A. "What does obedience mean?"
   B. DEFINITION: "Obedience is willingly, promptly, and cheerfully doing whatever an authority (such as Mom, Dad, Sunday School teacher, or God Himself) asks. It is also doing what you know that person would desire even if you haven't been specifically told." (Use an example, such as, "You don't jump on the furniture, even if I don't mention it every single day.")
      "Another word for obedience is SUBMISSION."
   C. Definition should be reviewed several times before moving on.

II. "This is what is expected of you:"
    (Following is a list of expectations as an example. Each family should draw up its own list of expectations, which should be clearly understood by all.)
    A. "You will obey Mom and Dad right away when told. We shouldn't need to tell you more than once. You won't forget if you do it right away."
    B. "You will be disciplined for not obeying the FIRST time."
    C. "We will pray together, and also separately, for strength to obey."
    D. "Mom and Dad will try hard not to yell at you or lose our tempers."
    E. "You will be expected to obey and submit to us without arguing."

III. "Why do we need to obey our parents?"
     A. "God says so."
        1. Read Ephesians 6:1.
        2. Read Colossians 3:20.
     B. "It helps us learn to obey God."

IV. Scripture study
    A. Read Ephesians 6:1-4 and Colossians 3:20,21 carefully and discuss.
    B. Memorize Eph. 6:1 and Col. 3:20 by saying together 5 times each.

V. Pray together for children to learn the habit of obeying promptly, and for parents to be fair and loving in disciplining.

DAY 2

I. Review
   A. "What is the character trait we are studying?"
   B. "Do you remember what our definition of obedience is?"
      (Thoroughly review the definition given in Day 1 lesson.)
   C. "What did we say would be expected of you?" "Of Mom and Dad?"

OBEDIENCE

DAY 2 (cont.)

    D. "Did you pray on your own for God's help in being obedient?"
       (Encourage children to remember to pray in their private prayer times for God's help in obeying.)
    E. "How did you do in being obedient thus far?"

II. Memorize Ephesians 6:1 and Colossians 3:20 by saying 5 times each.

III. Read Genesis 22:1-18.
    A. "What did God ask Abraham to do?"
    B. "Did Abraham argue?" "Did he obey immediately, or did he wait?" "How many times did God have to tell Abraham before Abraham obeyed?"
    C. "What was the result of Abraham's obedience?" "What did God promise him because he obeyed?"

IV. Pray that we could obey the first time we are told, like Abraham did.

DAY 3

I. Review
    A. Definition of obedience
    B. Memorization of Eph. 6:1 and Col. 3:20

II. Progress
    A. "Did you pray and ask God to help you be obedient?"
    B. "Do you have any victories (successes) to report?" "Any failures?" ("Did you ask forgiveness?")
    C. Thank God for victories and pray for continued help. Pray for Mom and Dad not to yell or provoke.

III. Read Exodus 3-4:20.
    A. "What did God want Moses to do?"
    B. "Did Moses obey God immediately?" (He argued.)
    C. "Why did Moses argue?" (He was afraid.)
    D. "Did Moses want to do what God said?" (no) "Did Moses do what God said?" (yes)
    E. "Obedience is not always pleasant, but it is still very necessary. Obedience always brings a blessing. Moses' obedience brought about Israel's freedom and God was glorified."

IV. Pray for obedient hearts that do not argue. Pray for help to obey when it is no fun.

OBEDIENCE

DAY 4

I. "How have you been doing with obedience (cheerfulness, willingness, promptness)?" "Have you remembered to pray for yourself at the times it has been hard to obey?" "Do you have any victories to tell?"

II. "Over the next few days we'll be learning about Jesus and how He obeyed."

III. Read Luke 2:41-52.
  A. "Can you summarize this story in your own words?"
  B. "Was Jesus obeying His Heavenly Father by being in the temple?" (yes)
  C. "Had Jesus done anything wrong?" (no)
  D. "How did Jesus respond when his parents wanted Him to come back to Nazareth with them?" "Did He talk back?"
  E. "Sometimes people might misunderstand and think you are doing something wrong when you're really not. It is important not to talk back. It might be all right to politely explain yourself, but you may not always have the opportunity. Remember that God knows your heart and He can take care of the situation for you."
  F. "What was the fruit of Jesus' obedience?" (verse 52)

IV. Bible verses -- read and discuss how they relate to obedience.
  A. Philippians 4:13
  B. Luke 22:42b. . .not my will, but thine be done.

V. Pray for ability to be subject to parents.

DAY 5

I. Review
  A. "What did we learn yesterday about obedience?" (Discuss previous day's lesson.)
  B. Discuss and memorize Philippians 4:13 and Luke 22:42b.

II. Read Luke 22:39-46, Matthew 26:39, and Mark 14:36.
  A. "What did God the Father want Jesus to do?"
  B. "Did Jesus find obedience in this situation pleasant?"
  C. "What did Jesus want more than His own comfort?"
  D. "Let's read Hebrews 2:9 together."
  E. "What blessing did Jesus receive for obeying?"

III. Pray together for obedience to blossom in our lives.

DAY 6

I. Memorize Phil. 4:13 and Luke 22:42b.

II. Read John 8:28,29.
  A. "Who was directing Jesus' life and actions?"

OBEDIENCE

DAY 6 (cont.)

   B. "What did Jesus say about His obedience to His Father?" (He always did what pleased His Father.)
   C. "We should make it our goal to let our lives be guided by the Holy Spirit, as Jesus did. We should want to always please the Father, too."
III. Read Mark 14:36 and review what is happening in this verse.
IV. Read Hebrews 5:7-9.
   A. "This Scripture passage is referring to Jesus' life on earth. Verse 7 is particularly talking about Jesus' prayer in the garden, when He asked His Father not to have Him die on the cross, if it were possible."
   B. "Even though Jesus was perfect in that He never sinned, He still had to experience what it was like to obey when what His Father asked was hard to do. Because Jesus experienced this kind of obedience, He fully understands what it feels like for us when we find it hard to obey." (verse 8)
   C. "When verse 9 talks about Jesus being made perfect, it is not saying that Jesus was imperfect, or less than completely good. It is saying that Jesus matured in His obedience through conquering His own will in order to submit to His Father's will."
V. Pray that we could be obedient, as Jesus was, even when it is very hard.

DAY 7

I. Memorize Phil. 4:13 and Luke 22:42b.
II. Read Philippians 2:5-11.
   A. "Verse 5 says, 'Let this mind be in you, which was also in Christ Jesus.' We are to be thinking as Jesus does."
   B. "Verse 7 tells us Jesus humbled Himself to be a servant. We should, too. If we see that Jesus did this it helps us to be cheerful and willing."
   C. "Verse 8 says He humbled Himself and became obedient. It is humbling to be obedient, but Jesus wants us to be humble. The opposite of being humble is <u>pride</u>. Not being obedient shows pride."
   D. (Verses 9-11) "What was Jesus' reward for being obedient, even to death on the cross?" (God exalted, honored Him; gave Him a name above all others; proclaimed that all would bow before Him and confess Him to be Lord; God the Father would be glorified.)
III. Have children copy the following Scripture references and read them again on their own. Encourage them to think about the Scriptures carefully as they read them. Smaller children may need an adult to read to them and explain what is meant.
   A. Luke 2:51
   B. Luke 22:42

OBEDIENCE

DAY 7 (cont.)

      C. John 8:28,29
      D. Hebrews 5:7-9
      E. Philippians 2:5-11

IV. Pray to be obedient to God (and to Mom and Dad), as Jesus was.

DAY 8

I. Review
    A. "What is the definition of obedience?"
    B. "Can you remember any times when it has been hard to obey, but Jesus helped you to do it anyway?"
    C. "Have you been remembering to ask Him to help you?"
    D. "Can you think of any of the Bible verses we've learned about so far?"
    E. Review and memorize Philippians 4:13, Luke 22:42, Ephesians 6:1, and Colossians 3:20.

II. Read I Samuel 15.
    A. "What did Samuel tell Saul that God wanted him to do?"
    B. "What did Saul do?" "Did He obey exactly?" "Did he obey part of what he was told?"
    C. "Was God pleased with partial obedience?" "Why not?"
    D. "When God tells us to do something, He wants us to do it just the way He says to do it. If we decide to do it our own way, instead of God's way, it is rebellion."
    E. "What reasons did Saul give for his disobedience?" (use animals to sacrifice to God -- v.21; feared people, so he obeyed them -- v.24)
    F. "What did Samuel tell Saul about this?" (To obey is better than sacrifice -- v.22.)
    G. "Can you think of any other Bible people we've ever read about who were asked to obey people instead of God?" (Peter and John and the other apostles -- read Acts 4:19,20 and Acts 5:29.)
    H. "What might have been other reasons Saul disobeyed?" (Samuel said he had become proud -- v.17 -- and rebellious -- v.23. His heart was cold toward God.)
    I. "What did Samuel say rebellion was as bad as?" (witchcraft -- v.23)
    J. "Did Saul realize he was doing wrong?" (yes -- v.21)
    K. "Would Saul admit that he had done wrong?" (No, he tried to blame the rest of the people -- v.21.)
    L. "What should we do if we disobey?" (repent -- admit we have done wrong and ask forgiveness)
    M. ."Did Saul truly repent -- was he truly sorry?" (No, he was only concerned about being embarrassed in front of the people -- v.30.)

OBEDIENCE

DAY 8 (cont.)

N. "What was the result of Saul's disobedience?" (God took the kingdom away from Saul -- v.23 and v.28)

III. Learn I Samuel 15:22b -- "Behold, to obey is better than sacrifice, and to hearken than the fat of rams." (The parent should explain again what this means.)

IV. "Just like God wants us to obey Him exactly, He wants children to obey their parents exactly. This is part of what it means in the fifth commandment, when it says to honor your father and your mother."

V. Pray for God's help to obey exactly.

DAY 9

I. "Do you remember whom we read about yesterday?" "What was Saul's problem?"

II. "Read I Samuel 15 again, silently." (Smaller children will need someone to read it for them, of course.) "As you read, ask yourself the following questions:
   A. Do I ever behave like Saul did?
   B. What does God expect of me -- to obey exactly, or is part obedience good enough?"

III. Have each child personally ask God to help him to obey exactly.

IV. Memorize I Samuel 15:22b.

V. "Remember when I said yesterday that God wants children to obey their parents exactly? This is part of the fifth commandment, to honor your parents. We are going to memorize the fifth commandment. Let's look it up in Exodus 20:12." (Proceed to read and memorize Exodus 20:12. Parents may also wish to review Ephesians 6:1 and Colossians 3:20.)

DAY 10

I. Memorize I Samuel 15:22b and Exodus 20:12.

II. Lesson application
   A. "When Mom or Dad tells you to do something, and tells you how to do it, should you do it a different way, as long as the main idea is accomplished?"
   B. "Is there ever a time this might be acceptable?" ("If you ask Mom or Dad very politely if it is O.K. to do your task another way or in a different order, and he or she says it is O.K., that would be all right. Most of the time, you should just go ahead and do as you are told, without discussion, however.")

III. Read Joshua 6:17-19 and Joshua 7.
   A. "Who disobeyed? "What did he do?"
   B. "What were the consequences of his sin?" (Point out that when we disobey, we hurt other people, too. All Israel suffered for Achan's disobedience. We may never know how many other people we hurt through our disobedience.)

OBEDIENCE

DAY 10 (cont.)

IV. Pray to be obedient so we don't hurt others.

DAY 11

I. Review definition of obedience.
II. Memorize I Samuel 15:22b and Exodus 20:12.
III. Read Hebrews 13:17.
   A. "Could you tell in your own words what this verse is saying?"
   B. "Who are the ones who have rule over you?" (Discuss this in the context of church authority and family authority.)
IV. Pray to be submissive to Mom and Dad's authority.

DAY 12

I. Memorize I Samuel 15:22b and Exodus 20:12.
II. Read Jonah 1 and 2, and 3:1-4.
   A. "Can a person ever hide from God?"
   B. "The men on the ship with Jonah would not have known Jonah was disobedient to God if he had not told them. Mom and Dad aren't always aware when you haven't obeyed exactly, either. But God always knows if you have obeyed or not."
   C. "Did Jonah's disobedience affect others?" "How?" (All the people in the boat were in danger from the storm.)
   D. "Did Jonah repent of his disobedience?" "How did God respond?" (He forgave Jonah and rescued him.)
   E. "What did Jonah do when God gave him instructions the second time?" (He obeyed God.)
III. Pray for grace to be obedient.

ORDERLINESS

DAY 1

I. "We're going to begin building another character trait in our lives -- ORDERLINESS. What does it mean to be orderly?"
   A. DEFINITION: Neatness, tidiness, accuracy, being on time. Orderliness means organizing our time and possessions; making the most efficient use of our time and possessions.
   B. "Orderliness can involve all types of neatness and good time use:
      1. Not daydreaming or playing when we should be working (thought orderliness).
      2. Keeping things put away in their proper place (cabinets, dressers, and floors not cluttered).
      3. Using our neatest handwriting and erasing well when doing schoolwork.
      4. Being careful to spell accurately when doing schoolwork."
      5. (Other areas of weakness the parent sees in his children)
      6. "What are some ways you would like to improve in orderliness?" (Be prepared for no desire whatsoever to improve. Kids generally love being messy. It's a whole lot easier than being neat!)
II. "We'll be taking a long time to learn about these things, and Mom and Dad will try to show you ways to make your life more orderly. It will take time. Even when we're done reading Scriptures about orderliness and talking about them, we'll still have to keep practicing orderliness. I want you to be sure to ask for God's help in your personal prayer time. Ask Him to help you learn orderliness. We can't change without the help of the Holy Spirit."
III. Pray we'll be teachable concerning orderliness.

DAY 2

I. Introduction
   A. "What is our definition of orderliness?" (See Day 1)
   B. "Do you remember why we want to build certain character traits in our lives? Our whole purpose is to become more like Jesus. We want to please Him. Since He is our perfect example, we should desire to have His qualities in our lives. Do you think Jesus is messy, or a time waster?" "Do you think the Bible could give us any ideas about whether God is orderly?"
II. Read Genesis 1-2:3.
   A. "What can we learn about God's ideas on orderliness from the Bible story of creation?"

ORDERLINESS

DAY 2 (cont.)

    B. "What would have happened if God had made the animals before the plants?" "What would have happened if God had made the plants and animals before making the dry land appear?"

    C. "We can see from the very beginning of the Bible that God is a God of order. This is a very big truth to know about God. Being orderly is an attribute (quality) of God's nature."

    D. "Just for fun, let's think about how things might have been different at the creation if God had not done things in an orderly fashion."

        1. "Did you ever stop to think how it would have been if God had placed the fish on land and the tigers in the water after He made them?"

        2. "God put everything in its special place. He made fish to live in the water, so He put them **in the water.** He made horses to live on land, so he put them **on the land.**"

        3. "We need to put things in their special, intended places, too -- the places which are best for those particular items."

III.   At this time, parents will want to explain their expectations for neatness. Clear, understandable rules, and the consequences of not adhering to those rules must be laid out. Start with just a few goals -- such as:

    A. All toys must be put in their proper places when you are finished with them (before dragging out more toys).

    B. Rooms must be tidied each day by a certain time (along with concrete examples as to what "tidy" entails).

    C. You may want to use an incentive program -- rewards for faithfulness in being neat.

    D. Each family finds different methods that are best for its particular needs.

IV.   Pray for grace in cultivating orderly habits.

DAY 3

I.   Review definition of orderliness.

II.   Read Proverbs 20:11.

    A. Discuss meaning of verse.

    B. Apply this verse to having a neat room, neat handwriting, etc.

    C. Memorize Proverbs 20:11.

III.   Discussion

    A. Talk about the old saying, "A place for everything and everything in its place."

    B. Discuss the many reasons tidy housekeeping saves time.

ORDERLINESS

DAY 3 (cont.)

IV. Optional -- provide a work time when parents help their children get their rooms tidy. Show them how to do various tasks, such as organizing toy boxes, dresser drawers, closets. Demonstrate making a bed properly, or folding clothes neatly.

   (Too often we assume that because we have shown children how to do these things once or twice, they now know how to do them. They do forget and need to have things demonstrated several times.)

   It is easier for children to get enthused about being neat if they can start with a neat room, rather than one that looks like a tornado tore through. Trying to bring order to a room that is already a mess can be too overwhelming for young children, making them discouraged before they get started.

V. Pray for grace to be orderly in keeping room clean. Remind children to be praying in their personal prayer times for God's help in being neat.

DAY 4

I. Review
   A. Orderliness definition
   B. Neatness rules parents have laid down for children
II. Memorize Proverbs 20:11.
III. Read Exodus 25:8,9 and Exodus 40:1-8.
   A. "God instructed Moses to have the Israelites build a tabernacle in which to worship Him. Were they to build it according to whatever design they liked?" (No, they were to carefully follow the pattern that God showed to Moses -- Ex. 25:9.)
   B. If your children tend to be careless with their handwriting or following your directions, this would be a good verse to apply. Show them the importance of doing things after the prescribed manner.
   C. Note that God gave a detailed account of how the tabernacle furniture was to be placed. Each item had its own special spot.
   D. "Just as God wanted the tabernacle furnishings to be placed in certain positions, our things should be kept in particular places also, so that:
      1. We can find them easily,
      2. They are well cared for,
      3. Everything looks neat."
IV. Read Leviticus 24:5-8.
   A. "What do you notice about God's instructions for the showbread?"
   B. "Do you think it would have been all right for Aaron to put the showbread in any random fashion on the table?" "Why not?" (God had given specific instructions for the order in which the showbread was to be laid.)

ORDERLINESS

DAY 4 (cont.)

        C. "God wants us to be orderly!"

V.   Pray for desire and ability to be neat.

VI.   Optional work time with parents demonstrating neatness techniques to children.

DAY 5

I.   Review orderliness definition.

II.   Memorize Proverbs 20:11.

III.   Read I Corinthians 14:26-40.
        A. Discuss the importance in God's eyes of orderliness in the church.
        B. Emphasize verses 33 and 40.
        C. Ask children to list points of order mentioned in this passage.

IV.   Pray for our local church to always operate in an orderly fashion.

DAY 6

I.   Memorize Proverbs 20:11.

II.   Progress review and evaluation
        A. "What are some things we have discussed about orderliness so far in our study?"
        B. "Are there any areas of your life where you are being successful at being orderly?"
        C. "Where do you need improvement?"
        D. "Have you remembered to pray for God's help in being neat?"
        E. Thank God for areas of success. Pray for help in areas where improvement is needed.

III.   "God has a special plan, or order, for each person's life. He has a way and a plan for you. Psalm 139:13-18 tells us about this." (Read in at least two different translations.)
        A. "Tell in your own words how this Scripture shows that God has a plan, or order, for you."
        B. Discuss verse-by-verse:
           1. V.13 -- God is in control of the development of each baby. He is protecting each one.
           2. V.14 -- the awesomeness of God's creation of each human being.
           3. V.15 -- God is aware of each baby and how it is forming as it develops in its mother's womb.
           4. V.16 -- "Unperfect" does not mean the same as imperfect; it means unfinished. God superintends each stage of each baby's development and even planned how each baby would look before it was ever conceived.

ORDERLINESS

DAY 6 (cont.)

        5. V.17 -- God is thinking about us all the time.
        6. V.18 -- He watches over us at all times.

IV. Thank God for having a plan for our lives. Ask Him to help us live according to His plan for us.

DAY 7

I. Memorize Proverbs 20:11.
II. Read Psalm 37:23.
    A. "Tell me in your own words what this verse is saying."
    B. "Isn't it neat that God has an order and a plan for our lives? Because He does, we can be confident He will guide us if we let Him. He is in control of all that happens to us."
    C. "How does God feel about the life of someone who knows and loves Him?" (He delights in him.)
III. Pray for God's continued help in developing orderliness in our lives.
IV. Optional work time together
V. This is the end of our study in orderliness. However, the parents will want to make sure that children continue to work at developing tidy habits around the home, in their schoolwork, in their appearance, etc.

DILIGENCE

DAY 1

I. Introduction
   A. "We're going to be concentrating on a new character quality, called DILIGENCE. Diligence goes right along with orderliness and Proverbs 20:11. What does Proverbs 20:11 say?" (Review verse.)
   B. DEFINITION: Working hard, carefully, and steadily. Synonyms -- industry, energy, thoroughness. (If you work diligently, you work with energy. You do your work thoroughly.)
   C. "These are areas in which we need improvement in being diligent:" (Note: these were areas we discussed in our own home, but each set of parents will have to decide what types of examples to use with their own children.)
      1. "Putting dirty clothes in the hamper, instead of in front of it. (This is doing work thoroughly.)"
      2. "Cleaning your room without stopping to daydream or play. (This is working steadily to complete the task.)"
      3. "Neat handwriting takes diligence. (This is working carefully.)"
   D. "Some opposites of diligence are laziness, carelessness, sloppiness, and not doing our work completely."

II. Read Proverbs 12:24, Proverbs 12:27, and Proverbs 13:4.
   A. "What is a slothful person?" (a lazy one)
   B. "How is the diligent person different from the slothful?"
   C. Read each of the verses again, discussing each separately.
      1. Prov. 12:24 -- "Diligent people tend to lead and to be put in positions of responsibility, but lazy people have to be supervised carefully, and kept in lower positions of responsibility, because they cannot be trusted."
      2. Prov. 12:27 -- "The lazy person is wasteful. The example given is that of going hunting, killing an animal, and then wasting the meat because the hunter is too lazy to dress and cook it. A diligent person does not waste. He does the work necessary to keep from wasting, or to maintain his possessions."
      3. Prov. 13:4 -- "A sluggard is someone who does not work hard. He may desire many things, but he cannot obtain them, because he will not put forth any effort to get them. Diligent people are willing to work hard to reach their goals, so they will prosper at what they are trying to attain to."

III. Pray for the quality of diligence to become evident in our lives.

DILIGENCE

DAY 2

I. Review Point I of Day 1, especially the definition of diligence.
II. Read Proverbs 26:13-16.
   A. "What is being said about laziness?" (A lazy person will make excuses for not working; spends too much time in bed; doesn't even want to work hard enough to feed himself; is wise in his own eyes, even though he can't give a rational reason for why he doesn't work.)
   B. "Is laziness acceptable to God?" "How do you know?"
III. Read Proverbs 14:23.
   A. "Put this verse in your own words."
   B. "People who feel it is necessary to talk a lot about all the great things they are going to do rarely accomplish much. All their energy is used up in talking about it."
   C. "It is difficult to work hard and talk at the same time. People who talk excessively don't get much done."
   D. "Working hard (diligence) is the opposite of being lazy."
IV. "What are some areas of your life in which you could be more diligent?"
V. Pray for the areas mentioned.

DAY 3

I. Review definition of diligence.
II. Read II Thessalonians 3:6-15 in two translations.
   A. "Who is saying that he is a good example of diligence?" (Paul)
   B. "How did he show diligence?" (did not behave disorderly, did not eat at others' expense, worked hard to support himself)
   C. "What does he want the Thessalonians to do?" (work hard to earn their living, discipline those who do not)
   D. "What were some of them doing wrong?" (not working -- but letting the other Christians support them, being busybodies)
   E. "What punishment was to be given if they didn't work?" (do not have fellowship with them, until they mend their ways)
III. Read Genesis 2:15.
   Discuss work as being something God always intended for man to do.
IV. Pray for ability to do work cheerfully because it is God's plan for us.

DILIGENCE

DAY 4

I. Review of II Thessalonians 3:6-15 material from previous day
II. Making work time enjoyable
    A. "Does God want us to enjoy our work and be happy while we're doing it?"
    B. "How could we make work time more enjoyable?"
    C. "Ephesians 5:18-20 gives us some ideas about how to enjoy our work." (read)
        1. Be filled with the Spirit -- the Holy Spirit fills us with His joy and peace.
        2. Speaking the psalms and songs -- God's Word fills us with joy and faith.
        3. Singing from the heart to the Lord -- also tends to make us joyful.
        4. Thinking of things for which to thank God, and expressing that thanks.
III. Memorize Ephesians 5:18b-20.
IV. Pray that God would help us remember Ephesians 5:18-20's instructions when we are working.

DAY 5

I. Review definition of diligence.
II. Ephesians 5:18b-20
    A. Review how this applies to working cheerfully.
    B. Memorize
III. Read Ecclesiastes 9:10.
    A. "What does this Scripture say about diligence?"
    B. "Should we be half-hearted in what we do?"
    C. "We should always take care to do our very best in whatever we are doing."
    D. Memorize Ecclesiastes 9:10a. (Whatsoever thy hand findeth to do, do it with thy might.)
IV. Read Daniel 6:1-5.
Discuss Daniel's diligence in his service to the king.
V. "Choose one area in which you would desire to become diligent. Work on it and ask God's help in improving. Be ready to report in one week on your progress."
VI. Pray for God's help in being diligent in this area of life. Pray to be diligent like Daniel.

DAY 6

I. Memorize Ecclesiastes 9:10a and Ephesians 5:18b-20.
II. Review previous day's lesson briefly.
III. Read Ephesians 6:5-8.
    A. "What does it mean to do something with singleness of heart?" (v.5 -- to be whole-hearted)

DILIGENCE

DAY 6 (cont.)

    B. "What is 'eye service, as men pleasers?'" (v.6 -- working only to impress people, such as a boss, instead of out of a sincere desire to do one's best.)

    C. Discuss opposing motives: pretending to work hard to avoid getting caught goofing off versus doing what is right out of love for God (doing the will of God from the heart)

    D. "When we are working, for whom should we really be working?" (God)

    E. "How will this affect our diligence?" (v.7 -- We will do our best.)

    F. "What is the result of diligence, according to v.8?" (God will reward us.)

IV. Pray that we could do our work diligently out of love for God and for love of doing what pleases Him.

DAY 7

I. Memorize Ecclesiastes 9:10a and Ephesians 5:18b-20.

II. Review Ephesians 6:5-8 by reading again and discussing.

III. Read Revelation 3:14-22.

    A. "What did Jesus say was wrong with the Laodiceans?" (They were lukewarm, not fervent in their love for Him.)

    B. "The Laodiceans were half-hearted in their love for Jesus. Were they diligent in their love for Him?" "We need to be diligent to keep our love for Jesus fresh."

    C. "Did Jesus give up on the Laodiceans?" (no)

    D. "What did Jesus tell the Laodiceans was the way to have their relationship with Him restored?" (repent)

    E. "If we fail in being diligent, in whatever area, Jesus will restore us through repentance and deciding to do right again."

    F. Talk about what is involved in being diligent to keep our walk with Jesus whole-hearted:

        1. Verse 18 -- buying gold of Jesus. Psalm 19:10 tells us God's Word is more desirable than fine gold. Proverbs 8:10,11 tells us to receive wisdom's instruction and knowledge (these come from reading God's Word) rather than silver, gold, and rubies.

        2. Verse 18 -- buying white raiment of Jesus. This speaks of keeping our walk clean -- making sure we repent of our sin regularly and asking God to convict us of sin so we can get right with Him.

        3. Verse 18 -- anointing our eyes with eye salve, that we might see. Being in touch with God gives us understanding. He guides us and gives us His way of looking at things as we are sensitive to His Holy Spirit. We need to spend much time in prayer, taking time to listen to God.

DILIGENCE

DAY 7 (cont.)

        4. Spending time with other believers -- Hebrews 10:25 commands us not to stop meeting with the rest of the church. This prevents us from falling into error.

        5. Sharing the good news of Jesus with others also keeps one's life in Christ fresh.

IV. Pray that we would not be half-hearted toward Jesus. Pray for diligence in seeking God.

DAY 8

I. Memorize Ecclesiastes 9:10a and Ephesians 5:18b-20.
II. Review lesson of Laodiceans' lukewarmness and how we can avoid this.
III. Read Revelation 2:1-7.
    A. Compare to Laodiceans.
    B. "Were the Ephesians diligent in working for the Lord?" (yes)
    C. "What was wrong?" (They had left their first love -- Jesus was no longer as important to them as He had once been.)
    D. Point out that it is important to be diligent in serving God, but we mustn't forget to be diligent in seeking His face out of pure love for Him.
IV. Pray for great diligence in seeking God for Himself.

DAY 9

I. Review definition of diligence.
II. Memorize Ecclesiastes 9:10a and Ephesians 5:18b-20.
III. Read Ephesians 5:15,16.
    A. Circumspectly -- cautiously, careful to consider all circumstances and possible consequences.
    B. Discuss thoroughly
        1. "According to this passage, how does a foolish person act?" "A wise person?"
        2. "What does it mean to redeem the time?" (use it wisely)
        3. "If we act circumspectly (carefully thinking about the situation and possible consequences), how should this affect our diligence?" (Talk about punishment as a consequence of wasting time when work is to be done.)
    C. Read Ephesians 5:15,16 again several times to begin memorizing.
IV. Pray that we would learn to use our time well.

DILIGENCE

DAY 10

I. Review definition of diligence.
II. Memorize Ecclesiastes 9:10a and Ephesians 5:15-20.
III. Review previous day's lesson briefly.
IV. Things to think about
    A. "What might be some consequences of using bad handwriting (not being diligent to write neatly)?"
        1. People may not get the right message, because they can't read what has been written.
        2. People may think you are a sloppy person in other ways.
    B. "What might be the consequences of taking too long to do your schoolwork?" (having to do it as homework)
    C. "How about housework?" (causing parents to be disappointed, having privileges taken away, other disciplinary consequences)
V. "Here are some hints for being more diligent to do your homework or housework:
    A. Keep tempting toys or books out of sight.
    B. Do homework at the kitchen table or a desk.
    C. Don't be in a place where other members of your family are, so you won't be distracted or tempted to talk.
    D. Play a game called 'beat the timer.' Set a kitchen timer for an amount of time reasonable for completing your tasks. Race against the timer.
    E. During housework follow Ephesians 5:18-20 -- praising and singing to God." (Say this passage.)
VI. Pray for God's help to use our time wisely.

DAY 11

I. Memorization
    A. Proverbs 20:11 -- This verse was memorized in the unit on orderliness. Review its meaning and apply to diligence before memorization review.
    B. Ecclesiastes 9:10a
    C. Ephesians 5:15-20 -- Discuss in depth again.
II. "Are you making progress in being diligent? Explain."
III. Read I Samuel 16:11 and I Samuel 17:34,35.
Talk about David's diligence to care for the sheep.
IV. Pray to be diligent in our own responsibilities.

DILIGENCE

DAY 12

I. Memorization
- A. Proverbs 20:11
- B. Ecclesiastes 9:10a
- C. Ephesians 5:15-20

II. Let children tell the story of Samuel's birth, if they are familiar with it. Otherwise, parent can tell it briefly. It is found in I Samuel 1.

III. Read I Samuel 2:11-17.
"Were Eli's sons diligent in performing the priestly duties in a right way?" (no)

IV. Read I Samuel 2:18.
Compare Samuel's diligence with Eli's sons' lack of it. Note this is second mention of Samuel's ministering.

V. Read I Samuel 2:26.
- A. "Why was Samuel in favor with God and men?" (One reason was probably his diligence to do well.)
- B. "Remember when we read in Ephesians 6 about not doing eye service as men pleasers? How does Samuel compare with that verse?" (He did his work wholeheartedly as unto the Lord. He was rewarded with God and men's favor.)

VI. Read I Samuel 3-4:1.
- A. "Does I Samuel 3:1 sound familiar?"
- B. "In verses 2-10, note Samuel's eagerness to be of service to Eli."
- C. Discuss again God's reward to Samuel.

VII. Pray for faithful, respectful diligence, such as Samuel had.

DAY 13

I. Memorization
- A. Proverbs 20:11
- B. Ecclesiastes 9:10a
- C. Ephesians 5:15-20

II. Discuss David's and Samuel's diligence and God's reward. Both were counted faithful in the performance of the small tasks that had been given them as children. Both went on to greater responsibilities in serving the Lord and their country. David became king, while Samuel became a great prophet and judge of Israel.

III. Together, list things in which your children are expected to be diligent. Among these might be obeying promptly and cheerfully, and neatness and promptness in household tasks.

IV. Pray about each of these points separately.

DILIGENCE

DAY 14

I. Memorization
   A. Proverbs 20:11
   B. Ecclesiastes 9:10a
   C. Ephesians 5:15-20

II. Read Genesis 39:1-6
   A. "How does Joseph show the quality of diligence in this passage?"
   B. "What happened as a result?" (He prospered in his work, his master prospered, and he was promoted.)
   C. "Was God pleased with Joseph?" (yes)

III. Read Genesis 39:7-20.
   A. "How else was Joseph diligent?" (He obeyed God.)
   B. "What happened as a result?" (prison)
   C. "Was God pleased with Joseph?" (yes)
   D. "Does being diligent always make things go well for us?" (no)

IV. Read Genesis 39:21-23.
   A. "How did Joseph respond to his situation?" (He was still diligent.)
   B. "What was the result?" (God prospered him, even in the prison.)
   C. "God is the ultimate rewarder of diligence. Things may get bad for a while -- even a long time. But God sees whether we are diligent under pressure, and He will reward."

V. Read Ephesians 6:5-8, and compare Joseph to this set of verses.

VI. Pray for ability to be diligent in difficulties, to be a God pleaser, rather than a men pleaser.

DAY 15

I. Memorize Ephesians 5:15-20.

II. Review previous day's lesson on Joseph.

III. Tell the story of the butler and baker's dreams, found in Genesis 40. The children may tell it if they are familiar with it.

IV. Read Genesis 41.
   A. "What wonderful quality, according to verse 39, had God developed in Joseph over all the hard years?" (wisdom)
   B. "As we are diligent, God can make us wise, also."
   C. "What did God do for Joseph because he was diligent?" (influenced Pharaoh to make Joseph the governor of all Egypt)
   D. "Was Joseph diligent as Pharaoh's governor?" "How do you know?" (He succeeded in gathering enough grain to feed all the people through the years of famine.)

DILIGENCE

DAY 15 (cont.)

V. Pray to be diligent in small and large things.

DAY 16

I. Memorize Ephesians 5:15-20.
II. Review lessons learned from Joseph's life:
   A. God will prosper those who are diligent.
   B. We must be diligent, even when things don't go the way we would like, and leave the results to God.
   C. God will not forget our faithfulness.
   D. Continued diligence brings wisdom and greater responsibility.
III. Read Luke 16:10-13.
   A. "What are the main ideas in these verses?" (Those who are given great responsibilities have already proven themselves by being faithful in small things. We must be single-hearted in our service to God.)
   B. "How did David, Samuel, and Joseph measure up to these verses?" (Discuss each separately.)
IV. Pray to be diligent to do our best.

DAY 17

I. Review definition of diligence.
II. Memorization
   A. Ephesians 5:15-20
   B. Ecclesiastes 9:10a
   C. Proverbs 20:11
III. Read Matthew 25:14-30.
   A. "How does this parable show us diligence?"
   B. "Who was diligent?" "Who was not?"
   C. "Does it matter whether God has given us lots to work with or not?" (no)
   D. "What does He expect?" (Do your best with abilities you have.)
   E. "What was given as a reward for diligence?" "What consequences did the lazy servant receive for his lack of diligence?"
IV. Thank God for all He has taught us in the diligence unit. Pray that He would make our new knowledge to bear fruit in our lives.

LOYALTY

DAY 1

I. Introduction
   A. "We're going to be studying the character trait LOYALTY. Can you define loyalty in your own words for me?"
   B. "Here is another definition of loyalty: faithfulness; being unchanging in our devotion to someone or something. A synonym is fidelity. The opposite of loyalty is unfaithfulness."
   C. "Name some people toward whom we should show loyalty." (Mom and Dad, other family members, eventually a husband or wife, friends)
   D. "Of course, our loyalty to God must come above every other loyalty, because He is first in our lives. Are there any others to whom we should be loyal?" (family of Christ, church leaders)
   E. Briefly discuss patriotism as being loyal to country; obeying of civil authorities.
II. "What are some ways we can show loyalty to:
   A. God
   B. Parents
   C. Husband or wife
   D. Friends
   E. Brothers and sisters in Christ
   F. Church leaders
   G. Country?"
   (Discuss each of these as extensively as you wish.)
III. Scripture memorization: John 15:13
   A. Look up and read together
   B. Discuss in light of loyalty
   C. Memorize
IV. Pray for God's help in learning to be loyal.

DAY 2

I. Review
   A. "Let's define loyalty." (Review definition from yesterday's lesson.)
   B. "To whom did we say we should be loyal, and what are some ways we can do that?"
II. Talk about the old saying, "If you can't say anything nice, don't say anything at all."
III. Scriptures about gossip -- look up and discuss:
   A. Romans 1:28-32 -- Focus on backbiters (gossipers) being worthy of death.

LOYALTY

DAY 2 (cont.)

      B. Psalm 15:1-3 -- Particularly discuss verse 3. Make sure children understand that taking up a reproach against one's neighbor means repeating gossip about him.

      C. II Corinthians 12:20 -- Emphasize backbitings and whisperings. Paul did not want to find that the Corinthian believers had been doing these things.

IV. "Gossip is a very terrible sin in God's eyes, and it is one we must guard against, because it is so easy for us to do. Gossiping is *not* showing loyalty. All of us need a lot of help from the Holy Spirit in being careful not to gossip or listen to gossip." (If this has been a particular weakness in your own life, your children are probably quite aware of this fact. Acknowledging your weakness before them and letting them know you will be seeking to improve will be a good way of teaching repentance and humility by example.)

V. "Let's pray for God to help us. Dear Father, please give us wisdom in our choice of words. Help us not to gossip, because we want to please You."

VI. Memorize John 15:13.

DAY 3

I. Review Scriptures from Day 2, Point III, rereading and briefly discussing.

II. Memorize John 15:13.

III. "If we're not to gossip, how are we supposed to handle our people problems? Let's see what the Bible has to say about this."

IV. Read Matthew 18:15-17.

      A. "What are we to do when someone sins against us, or hurts our feelings?" (Try to work it out privately with the person who has offended us.)

      B. "What should we do if the person who has hurt us will not admit he did wrong and ask forgiveness?" (Bring another person, such as Mom or Dad, into the situation.)

      C. "Some things you should always tell Mom or Dad about -- especially if it is a serious situation that affects you personally. For instance, if someone tried to harm you, or touch you in a way that isn't right, that would be something you should let your parents take care of. You should feel free to tell your parents when things have been said that hurt you inside, although it may not be important to say who said the mean things to you. Sometimes little arguments you might have with your brothers and sisters or friends are not important enough to come to Mom or Dad about, even if the person doesn't ask forgiveness. We don't need to be tattling on others all the time. Sometimes we just need to forgive and forget about it."

LOYALTY

DAY 3 (cont.)

    D. "Verse 17 is probably not going to apply to you at this time. It is talking about a Christian brother or sister being involved in very serious sin, and refusing to turn away from that sin. Most of us don't have to deal with this, but it is still important for us to know what God says about problems of this kind, so that we can do the right thing if the situation does come up in our lives."

V. "The <u>way</u> you tell Mom and Dad or other people about things that affect your relationships makes all the difference. Ask yourself first:
    A. 'Is it important for Mom and Dad to know this?'
    B. 'Is what I am going to tell about my own troubles with someone, or is it just about something bad the person did?' (Give an example.)
    C. 'Is what I'm about to say a put-down of someone?' ('Am I saying it to make myself look better than the other person?')
    D. 'Will I feel sinful for having said this?'"

VI. "Let's be sensitive to the Holy Spirit. Ask Him to show you if something is wrong to say, before you say it."

VII. Pray for sensitivity to think about whether what we say is gossip. Pray for conviction if we are gossiping, so we can stop.

DAY 4

I. Memorize John 15:13.

II. Review
    A. "What is loyalty?" (Review the definition of loyalty.)
    B. "How does John 15:13 speak of loyalty?"

III. "In our last few lessons we said a loyal person doesn't gossip. Gossip starts in the thoughts. If we let ourselves think nasty thoughts about people, often it leads to speaking gossip with our mouths."
    A. Read Matthew 12:34 and discuss.
    B. Read Matthew 15:18-20a and discuss.

IV. Read Numbers 12.
    A. "What were Miriam and Aaron doing at the beginning of the story?" (gossiping and backbiting about Moses' wife, then about Moses)
    B. "Who heard them?" (God) "Does God hear what we say about others?"
    C. "Why do you suppose they spoke against Moses?" (They were trying to build themselves up by putting Moses down.)
    D. "What did God think about the things Miriam and Aaron were saying?" (God was very angry with them.)
    E. "What happened as a result of Miriam and Aaron gossiping?" (Discuss the fact that sin brings consequences.)

LOYALTY

DAY 4 (cont.)

V. Ask God to teach us, through Miriam and Aaron's errors, not to gossip. Ask Him to put the lesson in our hearts, so we will not sin.

DAY 5

I. "What did we learn about yesterday?" "How can we apply this to our lives?"
II. "A loyal person sticks by the one to whom he is being loyal. Loyalty means we don't gossip. We don't think evil of the person. We believe the best of him that is possible. This doesn't mean we won't see his faults, but we stick by him in spite of his faults, and we don't broadcast his sins and shortcomings to others. We forgive and continue loving."
III. Read I Corinthians 13:4-7 in at least two translations -- using at least one modern language translation may be helpful. Discuss in light of loyalty.
IV. Memorize John 15:13.
V. Pray for loyalty to be a lasting quality in our lives.

DAY 6

I. Memorize John 15:13.
II. "Are you finding yourself more aware of how a loyal person should talk?" "Have you been catching yourself before starting to gossip?"
III. Read Ruth 1.
    A. "Who was loyal?" "How?"
    B. "Do you think it was always easy to be loyal to Naomi?" "Why not?" (homesickness, Naomi perhaps not always pleasant)
IV. Read Ruth 2.
    A. "Who was impressed with Ruth's loyalty?"
    B. "What was his wish for Ruth?" (He wanted God to reward Ruth -- v.12.)
V. Read Ruth 3 and 4.
    A. "How did God bless Ruth for her loyalty?" (gave her a husband, a son, she became an ancestor of the Messiah even though Israelites were never to marry Moabites)
    B. "Read Ruth 4:15 again. What did the townspeople say about Ruth?" "Was Ruth a blessing?"
    C. "People who are loyal are a blessing to others."
VI. Pray that we could be a blessing to others through our loyalty.

LOYALTY

DAY 7

I. Review
    A. Memorize John 15:13.
    B. "Whom did we learn about in our last lesson?" (Ruth)
    C. "Did Ruth fulfill John 15:13?" "How?"

II. Read I Samuel 18:1-4 and I Samuel 19:1-7.
    A. "What two ways did Jonathan show loyalty to David?" (Ch. 19 -- warned David and spoke well of him)
    B. "What was the result of Jonathan's actions?" (David and Saul were reconciled for the time being.)
    C. "Often, by defending a person and being loyal to him, we can help restore peace between people. Defending someone is a way of showing loyalty."

III. Pray for courage to defend people, when necessary, as part of being loyal.

DAY 8

I. Memorize John 15:13.

II. "Tell me what we talked about yesterday." (Review previous lesson briefly.)

III. Read I Samuel 20.
    A. "Whom did Jonathan defend in verse 2?" (Saul)
    B. "Jonathan was consistently a very loyal person. He tried to see every person in the most favorable light possible. This is a good quality to have. Remember when we read I Corinthians 13 a few days ago? I Corinthians 13 is talking about this kind of attitude when it says, charity '... thinketh no evil,' (v.5) and 'believeth all things, hopeth all things ....' (v.7)."
    C. "How did he show loyalty to David?" (warned David, again defended him to Saul)

IV. Read I Samuel 23:15-18.
    A. "How did Jonathan show loyalty?" (encouraged David)
    B. "How did Jonathan demonstrate John 15:13?" (was willing to give up the kingship to David)

V. Pray we could take Jonathan's example to heart and be loyal, as he was.

DAY 9

I. Memorize John 15:13.

II. Review
    A. "Who was loyal in our last couple of lessons?" (Jonathan)

LOYALTY

DAY 9 (cont.)

    B. "Can you list some ways in which Jonathan demonstrated loyalty?" (warned his friend, defended his friend and father, encouraged, set aside his own self-interest in favor of his friend -- concerning the throne)

III. Read Acts 15:36-40.
    A. "Who showed loyalty, and to whom?" (Barnabas, to John Mark)
    B. "Why didn't Paul want John Mark to go with them?" (He had not been dependable in the past.)
    C. "Was this a good reason?" (yes)
    D. "Why do you suppose Barnabas insisted on taking Mark?" (He wanted to give Mark another chance; he wanted to help Mark grow in maturity.)
    E. "Perhaps Barnabas had Mark's best interests at heart and wanted to help him. Which would have been easier for Barnabas -- taking Mark, or just going with Paul?" "Why?"
    F. "What happened as a result of Barnabas' loyalty to Mark?" (Paul and he had an argument and parted company.)
    G. "Is everybody going to be happy with us when we are loyal to someone?" (No, sometimes people may even reject us or make fun of us.)
    H. "It is still right to be loyal, even if it is hard. Sometimes the person to whom we are loyal will have messed up, like Mark had. We don't have to pretend the person is perfect, but we shouldn't let others cut him down. Instead, we could encourage people to give him another chance, as Barnabas did."

IV. Pray that God would continue to work loyalty in us, and especially that He would help us to not gossip.

DAY 10

I. Introduction
    A. "How is loyalty coming along in your life?" "Are you asking God to help you be loyal?" "What about gossip?"
    B. "Yesterday we talked about Barnabas being loyal to Mark. Today we'll be reading about someone who was loyal and someone who was not."

II. Read II Kings 11.
    A. Explain that Joash's aunt, who rescued him, was married to Jehoiada, the high priest.
    B. "Who was loyal to whom?" (Jehoiada, the priests, and the Levites were loyal to Joash. The Levites were special helpers in the temple.)
    C. "Was anyone loyal to Athaliah?" "Why not?" (The throne was not rightfully hers; she was unworthy to receive loyalty.)

LOYALTY

DAY 10 (cont.)

    D. "We don't have to be loyal to everyone. Some people are unworthy of our loyalty. But we still shouldn't gossip about them."
    E. "How did Jehoiada show his loyalty?" (by hiding Joash, raising him as one of his own family, rebelling against Athaliah to give Joash his rightful place as king)
    F. "Was there a cost to Jehoiada?" (Yes, he was risking his life by defying Athaliah.)

III.   Read II Chronicles 24:1,2.
"Joash served the Lord as long as Jehoiada was alive to influence him. He repaired and restored God's temple, which was in bad repair. But let's see what happened."

IV.   Read II Chronicles 24:17-22.
    A. "What happened to Joash when Jehoiada died?" (got in wrong crowd, turned away from God, became proud)
    B. "How did Joash repay Jehoiada's loyalty?" (with disloyalty)
    C. "To whom else was Joash disloyal?" (God) "How do you know this?"

V.   Memorize John 15:13.
Mention that Jehoiada lived this verse in his actions.

VI.   Pray that we would be loyal like Jehoiada -- even when it is risky.

DAY 11

I.   Review definition of loyalty
II.   Introduction
    A. "The most important person for us to be loyal to is Jesus. Our loyalty to Jesus must come before loyalty to any others. It must come before our own wants, needs, or convenience."
    B. "Can you think of any people who were loyal to Jesus?" (Mary, the sister of Martha; Mary Magdalene; Nicodemus and Joseph of Arimathea, at Jesus' burial)
    C. "Can you think of any people who were disloyal to Jesus?" (those that stopped following Him; Peter, at his denial; Judas)
    D. "All of Jesus' eleven remaining disciples proved loyal in the end; most were killed for preaching about Jesus."

III.   Read Matthew 10:32,33 and Luke 12:8,9.
    A. "What is Jesus telling us about being loyal to Him?"
    B. "Is it always going to be easy to confess Jesus and be loyal to Him?"
    C. "Sometimes people may reject us or make fun of us for being loyal to Jesus, but look what Jesus says about this in Matthew 5:11,12." (Read Matthew 5:11,12 and discuss.)
    D. "Who can help us be loyal to Jesus?" (the Holy Spirit)

LOYALTY

DAY 11 (cont.)

IV. Pray for loyalty to Jesus. Ask the Holy Spirit to help us be brave and to confess Jesus.

DAY 12

I. John 15:13 -- Explain that Jesus was speaking of Himself in this verse, and of His ultimate loyalty to us -- even to death.
II. Review the lesson from Day 11.
III. "We're going to read of two instances when the disciples were loyal to Jesus."
    A. "Turn to Acts 4:18-20. Peter and John had been arrested for preaching about Jesus in the temple. They had just been used by God to heal a lame man in the name of Jesus, and this had given them opportunity to tell about the Lord. The Jewish rulers now were questioning them, and did not want them to teach the things of Jesus anymore."
    B. Read Acts 4:18-20.
        1. "How did Peter and John respond when their rulers commanded them to stop talking about Jesus?"
        2. "How did their response show loyalty to Jesus?" (They obeyed Him more than men.)
        3. "How do you think God felt about their response?" (He was pleased.)
    C. "Turn to Acts 5:27-32. The apostles had been put in prison for preaching Jesus and doing miracles in His name. God sent His angel to open the prison doors in the night. The angel commanded the apostles to go to the temple and again preach Jesus. In the morning, the Jewish rulers sent for the apostles, and were astonished to not find them in the prison, but in the temple preaching!"
    D. Read Acts 5:27-32.
    "How is this incident similar to what happened to Peter and John earlier?"
    E. Read Acts 5:33-42.
        1. "What two things did the Jewish rulers do to the apostles?" (They beat them and commanded them not to speak in the name of Jesus.)
        2. "Do things always go well for us when we are loyal to Jesus?" (no)
        3. "How did the apostles feel about being beaten by the rulers?" (They rejoiced that they were worthy to suffer for Jesus. Relate this to what Jesus said in Matthew 5:11,12. Read those verses and refer to Day 11 lesson.)
        4. "What did the apostles do when they were freed?" (They preached Jesus in spite of the rulers' commands not to do so.)

LOYALTY

DAY 12 (cont.)

5. "Because the disciples had been baptized in the Holy Spirit, they were filled with His power. This is why they were able to be loyal to Jesus and to preach with boldness, although they were threatened. Jesus had promised them this power in Acts 1:8." (Read Acts 1:8.)

IV. Pray to be loyal to Jesus. If children wish to, pray for the baptism in the Holy Spirit. Emphasize that we desire His power and boldness so that we can be loyal witnesses for Jesus.

DAY 13

I. Read Hebrews 13:17 and I Thessalonians 5:12,13.
   A. "Can you put these Scriptures in your own words?"
   B. "What do these verses have to do with loyalty?" (We should honor the leaders of the church. We should never put them down or say rotten things about the pastors or deacons.)
   C. "We need to remember that God has appointed these people to have authority over us, and He wants us to respect their authority. If we have a problem with a decision they make, let's talk directly to them about it -- not drag our complaint to everyone else."
II. Memorize Hebrews 13:17 and I Thessalonians 5:12,13.
III. Pray that God would help us to always remember to honor our pastors and deacons in the way we speak of them.

DAY 14

I. Review
   A. "What did we talk about yesterday?" (Review lesson briefly.)
   B. Discuss the meaning of Heb. 13:17 and I Thess. 5:12,13, if necessary.
   C. Memorize Heb. 13:17 and I Thess. 5:12,13.
II. Read Numbers 12.
   A. "Do you remember reading this chapter before?"
   B. "How is this chapter connected with loyalty to church leaders?" (Moses was the leader of God's people, and he was being talked of in a bad way. His authority was not respected.)
   C. "How did God view Miriam and Aaron's behavior?"
III. Pray we would be loyal with our lips and in our hearts toward church leaders.

LOYALTY

DAY 15

I. Memorize Hebrews 13:17 and I Thessalonians 5:12,13.

II. "Yesterday and the day before, we talked about loyalty to church leaders. When you grow up, you may sometimes hear people criticizing the pastor or leadership of the church. You need to know that this is displeasing to God, so that you can avoid doing it yourself, and so you can encourage other people not to do it, either."

III. "A special kind of loyalty is called <u>patriotism</u>. Do you know what patriotism means?" (loyalty to country) "A patriot is someone who is loyal to his country. God wants us to be patriots.
   A. "When we say the Pledge of Allegiance, we are saying a promise of loyalty. Pledge means promise; allegiance means loyalty."
   B. (This would be a good time to review the Pledge of Allegiance, line-by-line, explaining any parts not well understood.)

IV. Read Romans 13:1-6. (If reading in King James, also read in a modern translation.)
   A. "Can you tell me in your own words what these verses say?"
   B. "What does God want us to do as patriots?" (obey laws of land, respect the governmental authority, pay taxes required of us)
   C. Talk about our loyalty to God being over and above loyalty to government. Give examples. Some examples from the past are:
      1. John Bunyan -- continued to preach and print Christian literature in defiance of the English laws which prohibited such behavior for those not ordained in the established church. He spent 12 years in prison as a result.
      2. Quakers -- just prior to the Civil War, they were mainly responsible for the underground railway, which helped runaway slaves escape to Canada. They did this in spite of a law which required all U.S. citizens to turn over runaway slaves to authorities so they could be returned to their masters. The Quakers could find justification for their disobedience in Deuteronomy 23:15,16: "Thou shalt not deliver unto his master the servant which is escaped from his master unto thee: he shall dwell with thee, even among you, in that place which he shall choose ... thou shalt not oppress him."
      3. Corrie ten Boom -- hid Jews from the Nazis. She endured imprisonment in a concentration camp in consequence.
      4. There are also many current examples of people who are standing for religious freedom in the face of oppressive laws. Stress, however, that one must make very sure to only disobey a law if obeying it would involve disobedience to God. Normally, we are to be law-abiding citizens.

V. Pray that God would give us wisdom about how to be good patriots.

LOYALTY

DAY 16

I. Review
   A. "What is a patriot?"
   B. "We've talked about some ways to be a good patriot. What are they?" (Review Romans 13:1-6 briefly.)
II. Read I Timothy 2:1-4
   A. "These verses tell us another way to be a good patriot. What is it?"
   B. "Why does God want us to pray for our country's leaders?" (for our own peace, for their salvation)
   C. Memorize I Timothy 2:1-4.
III. Pray for our country's leaders, as instructed in I Timothy.

DAY 17

I. Read I Samuel 24.
   A. "How did David show patriotism?" (He was loyal to the king, in that he spared his life.)
   B. "Why did David respect Saul's authority?" (verse 6)
   C. "Why did it bother David that he had cut off part of Saul's robe?" (verse 5 -- It showed lack of respect.)
   D. Read verses 11-15 again.
   E. "When our government authorities are unjust toward us, we can expect, as David did, that God will be the ultimate judge. He will bring forth fairness in the end."
II. Memorize I Timothy 2:1-4.
III. Pray for patriotic attitude toward our country. Pray for our government officials.

DAY 18

I. Review
   A. "We've been talking about the special type of loyalty we give to our country. What do we call loyalty to country?" (patriotism)
   B. "How did David show loyalty to the leader of his country?"
   C. You may wish to tell the story of I Samuel 26 -- another incident of David sparing Saul's life because he was the Lord's anointed king.
II. "Let's look at one more example of David's loyalty to his country's leader. Turn to II Samuel 1."
   A. Tell the story briefly. (A messenger has come to David with the news of Saul's and Jonathan's deaths.)
   B. Read verses 11 and 12. "How did David show his loyalty?"

LOYALTY

DAY 18 (cont.)

      C. Read II Samuel 1:17-27 and comment on David's praise of Saul -- also his loyalty as a friend to Jonathan.

III.   Memorize I Timothy 2:1-4.

IV.   Pray for our country to turn to God.

DAY 19

I.   Memorize I Timothy 2:1-4.
"What did I Timothy 2:1-4 tell us about being patriotic?"

II.   "Do you remember what we prayed for yesterday?" (our country would turn to God) "What does this have to do with patriotism?" (If we love our country, we will be concerned about its terrible spiritual condition. We will pray for salvation for America's people.)

III.   Sing <u>America the Beautiful</u>. (You may wish to go through it line-by-line and explain its meaning.)

IV.   Pray for salvation for the people of America. Pray for America's leaders, according to I Timothy 2:1-4.

DAY 20

I.   Memorize I Timothy 2:1-4.

II.   "Remember how loyal David was to Saul -- the leader of his country? Today we'll be talking about a man who was a servant of David -- Ahithophel. Ahithophel was King David's special counselor. He was very wise. He gave David guidance and helped him make decisions."

III.   "Turn to II Samuel 15. Absalom, David's son, has just revolted against David, and David is escaping from Jerusalem before Absalom gets there with his army."

      A. Read II Samuel 15:30-34 and II Samuel 16:15-19.

      B. "Who was loyal to David?" "Who was not?"

      C. "Why should Ahithophel have been loyal to David?" "Why was he not, in your opinion?"

      D. "Was Ahithophel a patriot?"

IV.   Read II Samuel 17:1-4.

      A. "What does Ahithophel want to do?"

      B. "Is he being loyal to David?" (Discuss betrayal and being a traitor.)

V.   Read II Samuel 17:5-14.

      A. "Is Hushai being sincere in his counsel to Absalom?" (No, he is acting as David's spy, trying to gain time for David.)

      B. "Was Ahithophel's advice to Absalom wise, or foolish?" (wise)

LOYALTY

DAY 20 (cont.)

        C. "Why didn't Absalom listen to Ahithophel?" (God caused him not to listen to Ahithophel's wise counsel, so that He could overthrow Absalom's plans.)

VI.   Read II Samuel 17:23.

        A. "What did Ahithophel do?" (He hanged himself.)

        B. "Why do you suppose he did this?" (pride at not having his advice taken; he knew Hushai's counsel would cause Absalom to lose, and he was afraid of what David would do to him.)

        C. "Ahithophel was not a loyal person. He only stuck with David as long as he thought it was to his advantage. He was only thinking about himself. A truly loyal person stands by his friends when trouble comes. He is not just seeking his own promotion or advantage at other people's expense."

VII   Pray for true loyalty, not just when it's to our advantage.

DEFERENCE

DAY 1

I. Introduction
   A. "Today we'll be starting a new character study -- DEFERENCE."
   B. DEFINITION: Showing respect and esteem to another person; honor. An antonym (opposite) would be disrespect, or possibly, bossiness.
   C. "When we show deference to someone, we submit ourselves to that other person's wishes, desires, or opinions."
   D. "When we defer to another's wishes, we make that person feel honored. It helps keep peace. When we defer (show deference) to others, we are being gracious. When we have friends over to our house as guests, we try to be gracious to them by letting them choose what to play -- at least part of the time -- and by offering them first chance to take a cookie or other snack. What we are really doing is showing deference."

II. Discussion
   A. "See if you can give me some examples of how to be gracious, or show deference."
   B. "Even if others don't show deference to us in return, we still need to act in this way."
   C. "When would be a time not to show deference?" ("We mustn't give in to, or go along with, something which we know to be wrong, or sense in our spirits isn't right.")

III. Pray for help in being deferent -- not bossy.

DAY 2

I. Review all of Day 1 material, especially deference definition.
II. Read Romans 12:10.
   A. "What does this verse have to do with deference?"
   B. "We are to show affection to others as brothers and sisters in Christ, but the part that particularly speaks about deference is, 'in honor preferring one another.' What does it mean to prefer one another in honor?" (to put someone else's needs, desires, or comforts ahead of our own)
III. Read Philippians 2:3,4.
   A. "Strife is fighting and arguing. Vainglory is glorifying ourselves, or bragging about ourselves. To be lowly in mind means not to think of ourselves more highly than we should. It is being humble, or modest. Esteem means love, hold precious, hold in honor."
   B. "Could you restate verse 3 in your own words?"

DEFERENCE

DAY 2 (cont.)

        C. "Is verse 4 talking about looking with our eyes at others' possessions instead of our own possessions?" (no) "It means we are not to think only of ourselves, but we are to consider and take care of the needs of others."

        D. "Tell me the phrases in these two verses that refer to deference." ('Let nothing be done through strife or vainglory,' 'let each esteem other better than themselves,' all of v.4)

IV. Memorize Romans 12:10 and Philippians 2:3,4.

V. Pray for grace to honor others -- to think of their needs first and not be bossy.

DAY 3

I. Review definition of deference.

II. Memorize Romans 12:10 and Philippians 2:3,4. (Review the meanings of these verses, especially any hard words.)

III. Read Romans 15:1-7.

        A. V.1 -- "We are to help those weaker than ourselves, bear with those who are not as spiritually mature as we may be, and not please ourselves (care for their needs first, put their comforts above our own)."

        B. V.2 -- "We do this with the purpose of building up the other person -- helping him to grow in Christ, or perhaps so that he will want to know Christ. Edification means building up."

        C. V.3 -- "Jesus is our example of deference. He did not please Himself. Instead, He pleased His Father first. And we can see in the gospels that He frequently also put other people before His own needs."

        D. V.5 -- "As God is patient and consoling (comforting), and as He has given us this example in Jesus, He wants us to be likeminded (thinking the same as He does) and treat others with patience and comfort."

        E. V.6 -- "If we are of the same mind as God, and are all together wishing to be as He is, this will bring unity to the Body of Christ and glorify God. By being deferent, you will be doing your part toward unity."

        F. V.7 -- "In what condition were we, when Christ received us?" (We were sinners, needing to be cleansed.) "How did Jesus receive us?" (He welcomed us and loved us unconditionally.) "This is how we are to treat our brothers and sisters in Christ; we are to accept them with all their faults, and love them unconditionally." (You may need to explain what doing something unconditionally means.)

IV. Discussion

        A. "Tell me what you have learned so far about deference."

        B. "How do you plan to apply this to your life?"

DEFERENCE

DAY 3 (cont.)

      C. "Are you being deferent toward your parents?"
      D. "Are you trying to be deferent in your dealings with other children?"
      E. Parents should share any experiences they have had with being deferent, not being deferent, or experiences of others being/not being deferent toward them.

V. Pray for God's grace to honor others and defer to their wishes.

DAY 4

I. Memorize Romans 12:10 and Philippians 2:3,4.
II. "In Matthew 5:9, Jesus said, 'Blessed are the peacemakers: for they shall be called the children of God.' People who are peacemakers often accomplish peacemaking by being deferent to others. Isaac was a good example of this."
III. Read Genesis 26:12-33.
      A. "What was Isaac's problem?"
      B. "Who was in the right -- Isaac or the Philistines?"
      C. "How did Isaac respond when the Philistines stopped up his wells?" "How about his response after he redug the wells and the Philistines fought him for them?"
      D. "What was Isaac showing?" (deference)
      E. "What happened as a result?" (God blessed him with much, including two wells and peace.)
IV. Pray to be peaceable people, as Isaac was.

DAY 5

I. Memorize Romans 12:10 and Philippians 2:3,4. (Discuss the meanings of these verses again, also.)
II. Review definition of deference.
III. "Are you improving in deference toward your brothers and sisters?" "Toward your parents?" "Toward neighbor children?" "Are you praying on your own for help in being deferent?"
IV. "In our last lesson, we talked about a man who was peaceable. Who was he, and what did he do?"
V. Read Romans 12:18.
Talk about difficulties your family might be having right now in getting along with each other or someone outside the family. Discuss ways the difficulties might be resolved, in light of deference. Perhaps forgiveness must be asked.
VI. Read Romans 14:19.
Discuss the importance of actively trying to live peaceably and building up others (encouraging). Make this a goal, especially for the family.

DEFERENCE

DAY 5 (cont.)

VII. Memorize Matthew 5:9. (This verse was mentioned in Day 4.)

VIII. Pray for the Holy Spirit to transform us into deferent people. Pray for grace to be peaceable in our home.

DAY 6

I. Memorization
   A. Romans 12:10
   B. Philippians 2:3,4
   C. Matthew 5:9

II. "In our last lesson, we talked about being peaceable and deferent within our home. How did we decide this could be accomplished?"

III. Read Ephesians 6:1-4 and Ephesians 5:21.
   A. "What do these verses teach us about having peace in our home?"
   B. "What can the children do to help the home be peaceful?" (obey parents, honor parents -- no disrespectful talk or face-making. Honor starts with the heart attitude.)
   C. "What can the parents do to help the home be peaceful?" (not provoke children -- through nagging; excessive teasing; negative, esteem-destroying comments)
   D. Ephesians 5:21 -- "We all need to submit ourselves to each other -- give up our personal preferences in favor of someone else, seek the well-being of each other."
   E. "Did you know that being peaceable shows we are flowing with God's plan for us? When we are peaceable, we are in tune with the Spirit of God."

IV. Pray for the peace of God to reign in our home.

DAY 7

I. Memorization
   A. Romans 12:10
   B. Philippians 2:3,4
   C. Matthew 5:9

II. Read James 3:14-18.
   A. "Where do envying and strife come from?" (the devil, the worldly way of thinking -- v.15)
   B. "If we have bickering in our home, where did that bickering start?" (v.14 -- in the heart attitudes) "Envying and strife (bickering) do not just pop out of our mouths: they start with selfish attitudes."
   C. "If we are fighting with each other, are we being deferent?"

DEFERENCE

DAY 7 (cont.)

    D. "What other problems are present when we are not getting along?" (v.16 -- confusion and every evil work)

    E. "Does this sound like a recipe for a happy home?" "Why not?"

    F. "Whenever we are acting in a way that Jesus would not act, it is not possible to be happy. We hurt others, and we hurt ourselves. We sin and hurt God, too."

    G. "God has a solution to this mess. Read verse 17 again. What is God's way to fix things?" (Emphasize being peaceable, gentle, easy to be entreated.)

    H. "When we are 'easy to be entreated,' we are agreeable, we listen to others, we don't demand our own way."

    I. "What happens if we follow God's way, as explained in verse 17? Look at verse 18 for the answer." (We will have peace in our home.)

    J. "Can you think of a word that would mean the same as being peaceable, easy to be entreated?" (deference)

III. Pray for God to work peaceableness, deference in our heart attitudes, in our home.

DAY 8

I. Memorization
    A. Romans 12:10
    B. Philippians 2:3,4
    C. Matthew 5:9

II. Review yesterday's lesson from James 3:14-18.

III. Tact

    A. "Part of being deferent and gracious is using <u>tact</u>. What is tact?"

    B. "Tact is the careful choosing of our words and tone of voice, so that we don't hurt people's feelings. A tactful person knows the right way to say something without causing offense. We all could use a lot more tact in speaking to each other in our home. Think of tact as being courteous in how we speak. Being tactful is a big part of being deferent, gracious, and peaceable."

    C. "Can you think of any time when someone was tactful in speaking to you?"

    D. "Can you make up some examples of situations where you could show tact to someone else?"

IV. "Today is the last day of our study of deference. What are some of the things you have learned?" (Discuss main points of the unit.)

V. Pray for greater tact in our family and among friends. Ask God to continue to make us deferent.

CHEERFULNESS (JOY)

DAY 1

I. "Our next character quality is CHEERFULNESS. What is cheerfulness?" "What would be some antonyms (opposites) of cheerfulness?" (grumpiness, complaining, murmuring, whining) "We will also talk about joy."

II. Read Nehemiah 8:10 -- last part only --" ... for the joy of the LORD is your strength."
   A. "What does this verse tell us about joy?" (It comes from God.)
   B. "What will the joy the Lord gives do for us?" (give us strength -- to do whatever needs to be done)
   C. Memorize.

III. Read II Corinthians 9:7.
   A. "This verse is talking about giving money for the Lord's work. What two ways are we not to give?" (Grudgingly -- grumpily; of necessity -- only because we have to)
   B. "How are we to give?" (cheerfully -- God loves a cheerful giver.)
   C. "How does God feel about cheerfulness?" (He loves it!)
   D. Memorize all of II Corinthians 9:7.

IV. "One thing Mom and Dad desire for you is that you be cheerful when you obey us. If you can't obey with a cheerful attitude, you are only obeying on the outside. You need to obey cheerfully from the heart, or else you are really being rebellious.

"There is a story about a little boy who insisted on standing on his chair, even though he knew there was a rule against it. After telling him to sit down several times, his father decided to get firm.

"'SIT DOWN!' he cried.

"The little boy sat down, folded his arms in front of him, and said, 'I'm sitting down on the outside, but I'm still standing up on the inside!'

"Of course, we know the dad should have insisted his son behave the first time that he was told, but the point of the story is that the little boy only outwardly obeyed. He was not cheerful in his obedience. He had not obeyed from the heart, but was still rebellious on the inside. That is the way we do not want you to be. We want you to obey from the heart -- cheerfully."

V. Pray for a heart that is cheerful about obedience.

DAY 2

I. "What is a good definition of cheerfulness?" "What are some opposites of cheerfulness?"

II. Memorize Nehemiah 8:10 (last phrase only) and II Corinthians 9:7 (all).

CHEERFULNESS (JOY)

DAY 2 (cont.)

III. Read Genesis 37:12-14.
- A. "What did Israel (Jacob) ask Joseph to do?"
- B. "Go back a little ways, and read Genesis 37:3,4. Joseph's brothers hated him and wouldn't even speak politely to him. Do you think it would be easy for Joseph to obey his father?" (no)
- C. "How did Joseph respond to his father? Did he whine or complain or grump?" (No, he went cheerfully.)

IV. Read I Samuel 2:11,18,26 and I Samuel 3:1-5.
- A. "Do you think Samuel was a cheerful servant to Eli?" "Which verses hint at this?" (v. 2:26, 3:4,5)
- B. "Why would it not be an easy thing to be cheerful in Samuel's position?" (He was away from his own family and might miss them, Eli's wicked sons might be hard to be around, a lot of work was expected of Samuel.)
- C. "Do you think God was pleased with Samuel?" "Which verse indicates this?" (v.26)

V. "Based on what you have read in the Bible about Joseph and Samuel, should you be cheerful when you are asked to do things for Mom and Dad?"

VI. Pray for a heart cheerful in obeying.

DAY 3

I. Memorize Nehemiah 8:10 and II Corinthians 9:7.

II. "What have we learned so far about cheerfulness?" "Have you been asking God for a cheerful attitude?"

III. Read Ephesians 5:15-21.
- A. "Do you remember this Scripture?" "Where did we learn it before?" (in the Diligence unit -- talking about how to make our work more pleasant)
- B. "Look at verse 17. What is the will of the Lord?" (to be cheerful) "Did you realize that it is unwise to be grumpy instead of cheerful? This is because anything that is out of God's will for us is unwise to do! We already know that God loves a cheerful giver, therefore, being cheerful is the wise way to be."
- C. "What does verse 18 tell us to do?" (be filled with the Spirit)
- D. "How do we go about being filled with the Spirit?" (We ask God to fill us with the Holy Spirit, and He will, if we let Him. God wants all believers to be filled with the Spirit, so that we can witness to others in His wisdom and power. If any of the children have a desire to be baptized in the Spirit, be sure to pray with them to receive this blessing sometime during this lesson. Encourage them that they can be filled, and should be seeking God for this. A basic explanation of the baptism may be needed if you have never discussed this with your children.)

CHEERFULNESS (JOY)

DAY 3 (cont.)

- E. "Verses 19 and 20 tell us how to be filled with the Spirit. These verses talk about praising God in various ways. When we are worshipping and praising God, our spirits are much more open to receive the baptism of the Holy Spirit."
- F. "Verses 19 and 20 also tell us how to be cheerful about tasks we are asked to do." (Read and discuss.)
- G. "How does verse 21 apply to being cheerful?" ("It is much easier to be cheerful when we are asked to obey, if we decide ahead of time to be submissive.")

IV. Review memorization of Ephesians 5:15-21.

V. Pray that God would give us cheerful hearts, full of praise.

DAY 4

I. Memorization
   A. Nehemiah 8:10
   B. II Corinthians 9:7
   C. Ephesians 5:15-21

II. Review of previous day's lesson
   A. "What are some things we learned from Ephesians 5:15-21, yesterday?" (Briefly discuss the main points, going verse-by-verse, if need be.)
   B. "If we are busy singing to God and praising Him, it is really hard to be grumpy at the same time, isn't it? Cheerfulness automatically comes with praising God."
   C. "Why do you think you should have a cheerful attitude about obeying and doing your work?" ("God wants us to obey, and it is also His plan for people to do work. We can be cheerful when we are in the will of God.")
   D. "Why is it a sin to whine?" (It is God's will for us to be cheerful givers -- II Cor. 9:7-- so whining is out of God's will for us.)

III. Pray for grace to submit without whining.

IV. Optional application of lesson
   "Today we are going to put Ephesians 5:15-21 into practice. We're going to clean your room (or whatever other household task is appropriate), and we're going to sing praise songs to Jesus while we're doing it."

DAY 5

I. Memorization
   A. Nehemiah 8:10
   B. II Corinthians 9:7
   C. Ephesians 5:15-21

CHEERFULNESS (JOY)

DAY 5 (cont.)

II. Review and assessment of progress
    A. "What is cheerfulness?"
    B. "What are some ways of acting that do not show cheerfulness?"
    C. "What does the Bible say about cheerfulness?"
    D. "What have you personally learned about cheerfulness?"

III. "Cheerfulness goes hand-in-hand with joy. Joy is one of the fruit of the Spirit."
    A. Read Galatians 5:22,23.
    B. "What is joy?"
    C. "We can have joy in Jesus, even when things go wrong, because He loves us and has saved us."
    D. Discuss the possibility of having joy in the face of troubles. Do this by talking about your own particular family's troubles and how Jesus can give us joy in the midst of those troubles. In our family, we were going through life-threatening health problems, so our discussion went like this:

        "Even though we don't know for sure what the future holds concerning Mom's health, and even though you're experiencing your own health problems, we can still be joyful. We have Jesus. He's much better than having our health, although He does want to heal us, too. Having health, but not having Jesus, doesn't bring joy. Only Jesus brings joy. And He gives us hope, too."

IV. Pray for joy in the middle of our troubles. Thank God for Jesus, our Joy.

DAY 6

I. Memorization
    A. Nehemiah 8:10
    B. II Corinthians 9:7
    C. Ephesians 5:15-21

II. "In our last lesson, we said we can have joy in Jesus even in the midst of troubles. James 1:2-4 has something to say about this." (read)
    A. "What purpose do trials have in our lives?" (make us patient)
    B. "God will work patience in us through our troubles. As we wait patiently for God's help to come to us in each difficult situation, we learn to trust God more. We become more mature Christians. For this reason we can even be joyful about troubles."

III. Read Psalm 138:8.
    A. "How does the Lord perfect us, according to what we just read in James?" (through difficulties)

CHEERFULNESS (JOY)

DAY 6 (cont.)

    B. "God is very concerned with making us more and more like Himself. He will help us to become complete, spiritually healthy people, and He may use trials to do it. We can take comfort in the last part of Psalm 138:8, though. God will not forsake us, because we are His creation. He will be with us, and will see us through all troubles."

IV.   Pray that our hearts would joy in Jesus and trust in Him in our troubles.

DAY 7

I.   Memorize Ephesians 5:15-21.
II.   Read Psalm 30.
    A. "What does this psalm say about joy?" (v.5,11)
    B. "What does it say about God helping us?"
      1. V.1 -- victory
      2. V.2 -- healing
      3. V.3 -- restoration
    C. "How does thankfulness relate to joy?"
      1. V.4 -- commanded to be thankful
      2. V.12 -- We should thank God when He brings us help.
    D. "Giving thanks will increase our sense of inner joy."
III.   Read Ephesians 5:20 and talk about giving thanks for all things -- how this causes joy.
IV.   Ask God to teach us to be thankful, bringing us joy. Thank Him for what we have learned today.

DAY 8

I.   "God has put lots of promises in His Word to encourage us in the hard times, so that we can continue to have joy. We are going to become familiar with two of these in order to increase our joy."
II.   Read Psalm 9:9,10 and Psalm 5:11,12.
    A. Discuss meaning of each and what reasons each gives for having joy.
    B. Memorize both.
III.   Have a special praise and worship time; give thanks.

CHEERFULNESS (JOY)

DAY 9

I. Review Psalm 9:9,10 and Psalm 5:11,12. Memorize.
II. Sing "Count Your Blessings," if you have a hymnal available.
III. Read Habakkuk 3:17-19.
    A. "What kinds of troubles are mentioned in these verses?"
    B. "What does verse 18 tell us we are to do, in times of trouble?" (rejoice in the Lord)
    C. "What will God do for us as a result?" (v.19 -- give us strength, help us live above our circumstances)
IV. Thank God for being with us in times of trouble. Ask Him for joy.

DAY 10

I. Memorize Psalm 9:9,10 and Psalm 5:11,12.
II. Read John 15:1-11.
    A. "Which verse mentions joy?" (v.11)
    B. "To what is Jesus referring, when He says, 'These things have I spoken unto you, that my joy might remain in you, and that your joy might be full?'"
    C. "If we abide in Jesus, we will bear fruit and be filled with joy. What does it mean to abide in Jesus?" (be like Him -- v.4; keep His commandments -- v.10; listen to Him and do what He says; depend on Him)
    D. "What will we have if we abide in Him?" (joy)
    E. "Who else will have joy?" (Jesus)
III. Ask God to help us abide in Jesus.

DAY 11

I. Memorize Psalm 9:9,10 and Psalm 5:11,12.
II. "We have much to make us joyful, even when circumstances go wrong. We can be joyful because Jesus said He would never leave us, and because the Holy Spirit lives in us and gives us comfort. Most of all, we can find joy in our salvation. Our salvation gives us fellowship with God, His protection, and the hope of heaven, with all its joys."
III. Read and discuss the following Scriptures:
    A. Psalm 35:9
    B. Isaiah 12:2,3
    C. Romans 5:11 -- 'Atonement' means that Jesus paid the price to wash away our sins.
    D. I Peter 1:8,9
IV. Thank and praise God for the joy of our salvation.

GENTLENESS (KINDNESS)

DAY 1

I. Introduction
   A. "Today we'll be starting to learn about a new character trait -- GENTLENESS."
   B. "How would you define gentleness?"
   C. DEFINITION: "When we are gentle, we treat people and things tenderly. We are soft-spoken. We show sensitivity and thoughtfulness in the way we act, and in the way we handle other people's feelings. When we are gentle, we are kind."
   D. "Gentleness is one of the fruit of the Spirit mentioned in Galatians 5:22,23. Let's look up that Scripture and say it a few times together to refresh our memories."

II. Application
   A. "What are some of the ways you think your parents could improve in being gentle toward you?"
   B. "What are some of the ways you could improve in gentleness?"

III. Pray that God would teach us to be gentle toward each other in the areas expressed in the above discussion.

DAY 2

I. Review
   A. "What is our new character trait topic?"
   B. "Have you been praying for the ability to be gentle?"
   C. Say Galatians 5:22,23 several times together to memorize.
   D. "What does gentleness involve?" (See Day 1, I, C.)

II. Jesus as our example
   A. "Can you think of anyone in the Bible who was gentle?" (Jesus)
   B. "Jesus is our best example of gentleness in the Bible. One of the ways Jesus showed He was gentle was by comparing Himself to the Good Shepherd."
   C. Read John 10:1-18.
      1. "How does verse 3 show the Shepherd's gentleness?"
      2. "How about verses 4 and 5?"
      3. "Verses 10 and 13 show us that gentleness involves thoughtful caring toward others: Jesus gives us abundant life. When we are gentle, we want to bring blessing to others."
      4. "Look at verse 15. Gentleness sometimes means we lay down our lives (our own wishes and desires) for others."

GENTLENESS (KINDNESS)

DAY 2 (cont.)

        5. "Does gentleness mean we are weak, or wimpy?" (no) "How do you know, from this Scripture passage?" (Verses 9, 11-13, 15, and 18 all speak of the Shepherd being strong -- keeping out the robber, fighting off the wolf, laying down His life.)

        6. "We can be strong, but very gentle. Jesus is very strong, but very gentle."

III.   Pray that we would be gentle and caring for others, like Jesus.

DAY 3

I.   Review
    A. Review meaning of gentleness.
    B. Memorize Galatians 5:22,23.

II.   "Yesterday, we learned that Jesus is gentle like a good shepherd. He cares for us tenderly and lays down His life for us. Isaiah 40:11 shows how gentle Jesus is." (Read and discuss this word picture carefully.)

III.   Read Psalm 23.
    A. Discuss in light of gentleness, verse-by-verse.
        1. Verses 1, 2 -- Gentleness cares for needs, protects.
        2. Verse 3 -- It restores, refreshes, and leads in right ways.
        3. Verse 4 -- Gentleness protects, builds reassurance, comforts.
        4. Verse 5 -- Again, it refreshes, brings blessing and gladness.
        5. Verse 6 -- Gentleness is tied to goodness and mercy.
    B. Memorize Psalm 23.

IV.   Pray for the gentleness of Jesus to take root and bear fruit in our lives.

DAY 4

I.   "Are you taking time in your personal prayer time to ask God to make you gentle?" "Are you becoming more aware of what gentleness involves?"

II.   Read Luke 15:3-7 and Matthew 18:10-14.
    A. "Notice that Jesus cares for each one of us as an individual, not just as part of a group. The <u>one</u> sheep that is lost, the Good Shepherd seeks after."
    B. "What does this tell us about how we should view people?" (Each person should be treasured and valued in his uniqueness, as Jesus would value him.)
    C. "How is tenderness shown by the shepherd in these Scripture sections?" (Luke 15:5)

III.   Memorize Psalm 23.

GENTLENESS (KINDNESS)

DAY 4 (cont.)

IV. Review points of gentleness from the Good Shepherd stories:
   A. Cares about individuals -- the shepherd in John 10 called each sheep by name; in Luke 15 and Matt. 18, he went after the <u>one</u> lost sheep.
   B. Is tender -- carries the lambs, leads the sheep with young in Isaiah 40; Psalm 23 -- leads to green pastures, still waters.
   C. Lays down life for others, defends others (John 10).
   D. Wants blessing for others -- abundant life -- John 10:10; Psalm 23 -- anoints with oil, prepares table, "surely goodness and mercy. . ."
   E. Creates trust in others -- like the sheep in John 10 can trust their shepherd.
   F. Is a comfort to others -- Psalm 23:4.
V. Pray we would develop these characteristics of gentleness in our lives.

DAY 5

I. "Jesus is our best example of gentleness. We've seen how he compares Himself to a good shepherd. Now let's look at some other ways Jesus shows gentleness."
II. Read Mark 10:13-16.
   A. "Do you think Jesus liked little children?"
   B. "What tells you this?"
   C. "Do you think the children liked Jesus?" "Why?"
   D. "How did Jesus show kindness and gentleness to the children?"
   E. "Many times grown-ups tend to ignore children and only pay attention to other grown-ups. They tend to think children are not as important. Was Jesus like this?"
   F. "Jesus was thoughtful of the little children's feelings, and of their mothers' feelings, too. Gentleness is thoughtful."
   G. "How does Jesus' treatment of children remind us of the Good Shepherd?" (Reread Isaiah 40:11 and discuss, compare.)
III. Memorize Psalm 23.
IV. Pray for gentle thoughtfulness toward those younger than ourselves.

DAY 6

I. "How did Jesus act toward the little children who were brought to Him?" (He was kind.)
II. "Paul, in his letters to the churches, also talked about being kind. Let's read in one of these letters to see what he had to say about kindness."
   A. Read Ephesians 4:32.
   B. Discuss the points made about being kind, tenderhearted, and forgiving.

GENTLENESS (KINDNESS)

DAY 6 (cont.)

      C. Memorize Ephesians 4:32.
      D. "What are some ways we can be kind and tenderhearted to others?"
      E. "If we try to imagine how we would feel in the other person's place, this helps us be thoughtful and kind."

III. Memorize Psalm 23.
IV. Pray for the ability to think how others feel, and act kindly as a result.

DAY 7

I. Read Isaiah 42:1-4 and Matthew 12:15-21.
      A. "What can we learn about gentleness from these verses?"
      B. Matt. 12:19 -- "Gentleness doesn't strive or cry; it doesn't make a big fuss. When we are gentle, we don't argue and fight (strive), and we are not unnecessarily noisy (crying in the streets). Gentleness is quiet and calm. Jesus was generally soft-spoken, not rough."
      C. Matt. 12:20 -- "This verse can give us a picture of how we should treat people. People who are hurting in some way are like the bruised reed. Jesus would treat these people with particular gentleness. He wouldn't be careless of their feelings and break their hearts further. He wouldn't squelch or quench them by stepping all over their feelings. We shouldn't do that either."
      D. Matt. 12:21 -- "What is the result of being gentle and tenderhearted, or thoughtful, toward others?" (It creates trust in their hearts. This is why we trust Jesus -- we know He really cares.)

II. Memorize Ephesians 4:32 and Psalm 23.
III. Pray for thoughtfulness and sensitivity to others, such as Jesus showed.

DAY 8

I. "One of the things that shows gentleness is having compassion. What is compassion?" (entering into the sufferings of another in order to help him)
II. Read Luke 10:25-37.
      A. "Who showed compassion?" "Who did not?"
      B. "How did the Samaritan show compassion?" (bound up wounds, gave up his donkey to hurt man, gave up his own time, gave his money for man's care)
      C. "What is another word to describe the Good Samaritan's compassion?" (v.37 -- mercy)
      D. "What can the Good Samaritan story teach us about how we should behave?"
      E. "Gentleness cares for, and has compassion on, others."

GENTLENESS (KINDNESS)

DAY 8 (cont.)

III. Memorize Psalm 23 and Ephesians 4:32.
IV. Pray that God would teach us to be compassionate.

DAY 9

I. Review
    A. "What was our lesson about yesterday?"
    B. "What is compassion?"
    C. "Can you think of any examples of compassion being shown in the Bible?"
II. Read Mark 1:40-42.
    A. "What was the man's problem?"
    B. "What was Jesus' inner response to the man's need?" (moved with compassion)
    C. "How did Jesus show His compassion?" (He touched the man. Discuss how much this must have meant to the man. Jesus healed him.)
    D. "Compassion feels with a hurting person and acts to help. Compassion also wants the best for that person. Jesus said, 'I will; be thou clean.'"
    E. "We need to realize that compassion always costs us something. It means giving of ourselves, even when it is not convenient or comfortable. This is the way Jesus gives to us, and it is the way He expects us to give to others."
III. Memorize Psalm 23 and Ephesians 4:32.
IV. Pray for hearts of compassion toward others in need.

DAY 10

I. Memorize Psalm 23 and Ephesians 4:32.
II. "There is another Scripture, much like Ephesians 4:32, which talks about some aspects of gentleness. Let's read Colossians 3:12-14."
    A. "What phrases describe gentleness?" (bowels of mercy -- speaks of compassion, kindness, meekness, long-suffering [patience], forbearing [putting up with others], forgiving, putting on charity [being loving in action])
    B. Discuss each of the above phrases in detail, in light of gentleness.
III. Pray that God would work these qualities in us.

DAY 11

I. Review definition of gentleness.
II. "What are some ways we can show kindness?" (List as many ways as the children can think of. Make sure these are real, practical things we can do. Have each child choose two of these ideas and make an effort to act them out in real life this week.)

GENTLENESS (KINDNESS)

DAY 11 (cont.)

III. Read I Corinthians 13:4.
    A. Go through this verse phrase-by-phrase, putting into modern English for the children. You may want to look it up in one or two modern translations.
    B. Memorize I Corinthians 13:4.
IV. Pray that God would help us be more aware of how to be kind to others.

DAY 12

I. Remind about two acts of kindness chosen in previous lesson.
II. Memorize I Corinthians 13:4.
III. Read Luke 6:35,36.
    A. "What do these verses have to say about kindness?"
    B. "Whom will we be like if we are kind?" (our Heavenly Father)
    C. "To whom is God our Father kind?" (the unthankful and evil)
    D. "Is it easy for us to be kind to those who don't like us?"
    E. "What can we do when it is hard to be kind?" (ask for God's help and strength)
IV. Read Luke 6:27-36.
    A. "Tell me all the ways that Jesus mentions that we can be kind to those who are not kind to us." (Among those listed are loving enemies, doing good to those who hate us, praying for those that are unkind to us, not retaliating, treating others as we would want to be treated.)
    B. "Verses 32-34 point out that even unbelievers love when they are loved, and do good when they will get something in return from those to whom they are good, but are we who love Jesus to be motivated in these ways?" (no)
    C. "According to verses 35 and 36, why are we to be good to others?" (because God is good to those who don't love Him, simply because He loves being merciful. He will eventually reward us for being like Him.)
V. Pray for grace to be kind, even in difficult situations.

DAY 13

I. Memorize I Corinthians 13:4.
II. Review lesson from Luke 6:27-36.
III. Read Proverbs 31:26.
    A. Explain that this verse is in the middle of a section that describes a godly woman.
    B. Talk about using our tongues with kindness -- kind words, refraining from unkind words, kind tone of voice making all the difference.

GENTLENESS (KINDNESS)

DAY 13 (cont.)

IV. Read Proverbs 31:10-12.
Discuss how the woman is kind to her husband, and how this could be applied to all our family relationships. For instance, family members should be able to trust each other and be confident that the other members will be loyal to them. They should do good to each other, not evil. Kindness is hardest to consistently live out in a family setting. How we behave toward family members is the true test of whether we are really kind.

V. Read Proverbs 31:20.
"How does this verse illustrate kindness?" (helping the poor and needy)

VI. Memorize Proverbs 31:26.

VII. Pray for kindness in the use of our tongues, particularly toward family members.

DAY 14

I. Remind about the two acts of kindness that are to be done. If any of the children are ready to share what they did to be kind, allow time for sharing.

II. "What did we learn about yesterday?" (Review kindness in the use of the tongue.)

III. Memorize Proverbs 31:26 and I Corinthians 13:4.

IV. "We talked a few days ago about being kind to those who aren't nice to us. Let's read another Scripture on the same subject. Turn to Romans 12:20,21."
   A. "What does God tell us to do?"
   B. "Give me some examples of how we could carry this out in our everyday lives."
   C. "What does verse 21 say to us?"
   D. "The Bible tells us in several places, such as I John 5:4,5, that we are to be overcomers through the power that Christ gives us. This is how we can overcome evil with good. Let's read I John 5:4,5."

V. Pray for awareness of how to be kind. Thank God for all He has taught us in the gentleness/kindness unit. Ask Him to make what we have studied bear fruit in our lives.

CONTENTMENT

DAY 1

I. Introduction
   A. "Our new character study will be on CONTENTMENT. What is contentment?"
   B. DEFINITION: Choosing to be satisfied and at peace with what God has provided, without complaining.
   C. "We'll also be talking a little later about gratitude. God wants us to be happy with what we have, and grateful to Him for providing it."
II. "In the Bible, God has many things to say about being content."
   A. Read Philippians 4:11b and discuss. (Make sure younger children understand that "in whatsoever state I am" does not refer to a location, but to a condition of being.)
   B. Memorize Philippians 4:11b.
III. "Can you think of any Bible characters who demonstrated contentment?" "How did they show they were content?"
   A. Paul -- wrote Phil. 4:11.
   B. Daniel -- made the best of his captivity and served God and the king to the fullest.
   C. Esau, in his later years -- initially refused Jacob's gift, saying he had enough things. (Genesis 33:9)
   D. Jesus -- was content even though He said the Son of Man had nowhere to lay His head.
IV. Pray that God would teach us deep down in our hearts to be content.

DAY 2

I. Review
   A. "Which character trait are we studying?"
   B. "Do you remember our definition of contentment?" (Review definition, Day 1, I, B.)
   C. "Do you remember any Bible characters who showed contentment, and how they did it?"
   D. Memorize Philippians 4:11b.
   E. "Today we'll be looking at some other things God had to say about contentment."
II. Read I Timothy 6:6-11.
   A. V.6 -- "Why would godliness with contentment bring us great gain?" (Contentment brings peace in our hearts. We can concentrate our energies on God's work, rather than on getting things.)

CONTENTMENT

DAY 2 (cont.)

- B. V.7 -- Discuss the fact that riches do not follow to the grave. Job said, "Naked came I out of my mother's womb, and naked shall I return thither. . . ." (Job 1:21)
- C. V.8 -- Discuss in light of the needy around the world who don't even have these things
- D. V.9 -- "How do you think desiring to be rich could lead us into temptation and destroy us?" (causing our focus and love to be removed from Jesus, causing our energies to be spent on things having no eternal value, tempting us to do dishonest things, bringing worry)
- E. V.10 -- Discuss how this verse is often misquoted. It does not say money is the root of all evil, but the <u>love</u> of money.
    1. Coveting money and material goods often causes one to err from the faith. Discuss the wrong prosperity teaching that one's financial success is a direct indicator of one's spirituality (teaching that says if a person is not rich in earthly goods, there is something wrong with his relationship with God).
    2. "What kind of sorrows could result from loving money?" (sorrow of financial ruin, sorrow of losing intimate relationship with Jesus)
- F. V.11 -- "What does God say we are to do instead of seeking riches?"

III. Begin memorizing I Timothy 6:6-11 by reading aloud together once or twice each day.

IV. Pray that God would work the joy of contentment in our lives.

DAY 3

I. Review definition of contentment.

II. Memorize Philippians 4:11b and I Timothy 6:6-11.

III. "Let's talk more about some of the concepts we discovered yesterday in I Timothy 6:6-11."
- A. Read I Timothy 6:6 again.
- B. Read Philippians 3:7,8.
- C. "Knowing Jesus is the greatest gain of all. Paul was willing to give up all things in order to know Christ fully. His passion for Jesus made everything else, in comparison, as nothing. We must have passion for Jesus like this also."

IV. Pray that our great passion would be Jesus alone.

CONTENTMENT

DAY 4

I. Memorize Philippians 4:11b and I Timothy 6:6-11.
II. Read I Timothy 6:7 again.
   A. "Jesus gives us a parable that illustrates this verse well. Turn to Luke 12:13-21."
   B. Read and discuss Luke 12:13-21.
      1. "What problem was Jesus warning against in this parable?" (covetousness -- loving things and wanting more of them)
      2. "What was the rich farmer's mistake?" (trusting in his riches instead of trusting in God)
      3. "What happened to the rich man?" (He died and left his riches behind.)
      4. "What did God call the man who trusted in his riches?" (a fool)
      5. "What did Jesus say we should do instead?" (be rich toward God)
      6. "How might we be rich toward God?"
      7. "Read I Timothy 6:7 again. What does the parable we just read have to do with this verse?"
III. Pray that we would be content -- not greedy for more, but rich toward God.

DAY 5

I. Memorize Philippians 4:11b and I Timothy 6:6-11.
II. Read I Timothy 6:7 again.
   A. "Because we can't carry earthly riches with us when we die, what should we do about our riches? Jesus gives us an answer to this."
   B. Read Matthew 6:19-21.
      "What are some ways we can lay up our treasure in heaven?" (bring others to Jesus, use our money for God's purposes -- such as supporting missions. Love for God and prayer according to God's will also become treasure in heaven.)
   C. "Let's look at another Scripture that tells us what to do because we can't take earthly treasures with us when we die. We're going to read Colossians 3:1-4." (read)
      1. "If we are saved -- 'risen with Christ' -- what are we to do?" (v.1)
      2. "What does verse 2 tell us to do?"
      3. "Why?" (v.3) "What does verse 3 mean?" (We are to be as uninterested as dead men would be in the things of this world, but alive to Christ and heavenly things.)
      4. "What promise does verse 4 give us?" (When Jesus returns to earth to rule, we will be coming back with Him in glory.)
      5. "We will have glory and riches beyond imagination when we are with Jesus."
III. Pray that God would daily show us how to lay up treasure in heaven. Pray that He will help us "set our affections on things above, not on the earth."

CONTENTMENT

DAY 6

I. Memorize Philippians 4:11b and I Timothy 6:6-11.
II. Read I Timothy 6:8 again.
    A. "Can you remember any teachings Jesus gave, which might go along with this verse?
    B. Read Matthew 6:25-34.
        1. "What two things does Jesus say our Father will provide?"
        2. "Look at I Timothy 6:8 again. With what two things are we to be content?"
        3. "What other things might be necessities for life that we could expect God to provide?" (shelter in cold climates, water)
        4. "What doesn't Jesus want us to do concerning food and clothes?" (worry)
        5. "What does God promise in verse 33?" "This concerns the 'extras' we may desire, too. What condition is attached to the promise?" (We must seek God's kingdom and His righteousness first.) "We must have a passion for Jesus first."
III. Thank God for promising to meet our needs. Ask His help in being content and putting Him first.

DAY 7

I. Memorize Philippians 4:11b and I Timothy 6:6-11.
II. Read I Timothy 6:8 again.
"There are some passages in Proverbs and in Hebrews that also speak about being content with what we have." (Read and discuss the following verses.)
    A. Proverbs 15:16,17
    B. Proverbs 16:8
    C. Proverbs 17:1
    D. Proverbs 30:7-9
    E. Hebrews 13:5 -- "conversation," in the King James Version, means lifestyle.
III. Memorize Hebrews 13:5.
IV. Pray that God would help us to be content with the things we have -- and to be thankful, too.

DAY 8

I. Memorization
    A. Philippians 4:11b
    B. Hebrews 13:5 -- review meanings of "conversation" and "covetousness," if necessary.
    C. I Timothy 6:6-11

CONTENTMENT

DAY 8 (cont.)

II. Read I Timothy 6:9,10.
"We will be looking at some other Scripture verses that go along with these verses in Timothy."
  A. Read Psalm 62:10.
    1. Explain any hard to understand words, such as "oppression" and "vain."
    2. Discuss the main thought of the verse.
    3. "People who are greedy to get rich often fall into the temptation to oppress -- or step all over -- other people to get rich. They might be tempted to be dishonest."
    4. "God never says it is a sin to have riches or things; He just doesn't want us to have our hearts wrapped up in them."
  B. Read Proverbs 15:27.
    1. "Greedy people often have unhappy homes. Their loved ones feel neglected, because money-making takes up all their thoughts and time."
    2. "A person who loves money might be tempted to take bribes and be dishonest. Money-lovers are willing to sell their honor if the bribe is high enough. 'Gifts' means bribes, in this verse."
III. Pray that God would keep us from being attached to money and what it can buy.

DAY 9

I. Memorization
  A. Philippians 4:11b
  B. Hebrews 13:5
  C. I Timothy 6:6-11
II. Read I Timothy 6:9,10.
  A. Read Proverbs 23:4,5.
    1. "In man's own natural wisdom, striving for riches seems good, but this is a way the devil ensnares people."
    2. "The economy of a whole country can collapse very quickly, or a person's business can fail overnight. Riches are never something one should put his trust in. They can disappear so quickly."
  B. Read Proverbs 28:20-22.
    1. "What does God promise a faithful person?"
    2. "How might a person that is hasty to be rich not be innocent?"
    3. "What is respect of persons?" (playing favorites)
    4. "Verse 21 warns us that those who love money will sell their integrity (honor) for money or material possessions. They will sin to gain what they want."

CONTENTMENT

DAY 9 (cont.)

       5. "Why might poverty come to the greedy, covetous person?" (God cannot bless covetousness.)

       6. "Even if a person who loves money does not lose his riches in this life, he will have nothing when he stands before God. Remember what Jesus said, 'For what is a man profited, if he shall gain the whole world, and lose his own soul?'" (Matthew 16:26)

   C. "What are some ways we have seen today that the love of money is the root of all evil?"

III. Pray God to keep our hearts and minds fastened on Him -- not on things.

DAY 10

I. Memorization
   A. Philippians 4:11b
   B. Hebrews 13:5
   C. I Timothy 6:6-11

II. Read I Timothy 6:9,10.
   A. Read Proverbs 21:6.
       1. "What is the sin mentioned, which is connected with love of money?"
       2. "What reward is promised to those who act this way?" (death)
   B. Read Proverbs 22:1.
       1. "What is more important than having riches?" (a good reputation)
       2. "Why do you think people who strive to be rich often do not have a good reputation?" (They hurt others to get their money; they are dishonest in their dealings.)
       3. "Does this mean it is bad to be rich?" (No, it is only bad if you love money, because then you might be dishonest in order to get more. It's fine to have money if you use it in a way that pleases God -- for God's glory.)
   C. "The biggest sorrow a person causes himself by loving riches is losing Jesus." (Read Matthew 6:24 and Matthew 16:26 together and discuss.)

III. Pray for the joy and peace of being content with what we have. Pray we would not be too attached to our possessions.

DAY 11

I. Memorization
   A. Philippians 4:11b
   B. Hebrews 13:5
   C. I Timothy 6:6-11

CONTENTMENT

DAY 11 (cont.)

II. Read I Timothy 6:11.
"What are things we should flee, and how do we do it?" (by following after righteousness, godliness, faith, love, patience, and meekness)

III. Read I John 2:15-17.
  A. Discuss bit-by-bit.
  B. "How does this relate to being content?"
  C. "What things are mentioned from which God would want us to flee?"
  D. "To be coveting things we don't have, or thinking the things we do have give us value, is loving the world. These verses tell us we can't love the world and love God, too. It is one or the other. We can't have it both ways."
  E. "What might be a way we could avoid lusting with our eyes?" (There are so many answers to this question, depending on the individual's particular weaknesses. For instance, for some children, a spirit of discontent is cultivated every time they visit a toy department at the local store, even though the original intent was "just to look." For a child that has a problem with this, avoiding the toy department would ward off the temptation of lusting with the eyes.)

IV. Memorize I John 2:15-17.

V. Pray that God would help us flee from lusting after things.

DAY 12

I. Memorization
  A. Hebrews 13:5
  B. I John 2:15-17
  C. I Timothy 6:6-11

II. Read and review I Timothy 6:11 briefly.

III. Read James 4:1-5.
  A. "According to James, why do Christians fight among themselves?" (lust for things, envy)
  B. "Why didn't God give these Christians what they desired?" (They lusted and envied, rather than asking God, or they asked for selfish, lustful reasons, instead of out of real need, instead of out of desire for God's glory.)
  C. "What did God call them because of their selfish desires?" (adulterers, because God was not their first love)
  D. "What did God say about our relationship with Him, if we are friends of the world?" (We are His enemies.)
  E. "What does it mean to be friends of the world?"

IV. Pray that we would be God's friends -- not friends of the world.

CONTENTMENT

DAY 13

I. Review contentment definition.
II. Memorization
    A. Hebrews 13:5
    B. I Timothy 6:6-11
    C. I John 2:15-17
III. "There is really no need for us to covet things, or strive for riches, or be worried about having enough. God loves to give His children good things. He has promised over and over in His Word to give us what we need -- and more. God is never stingy."
IV. Read Philippians 4:19.
    A. "How much of our need has God promised to give?" (all)
    B. "Is there a limit to how much God is able to give?" (no) "Which words in the verse tell us this?" (all, according to his riches in glory)
V. Read Psalm 68:19.
    A. "Tell me what this verse says, in your own words."
    B. "How often does God bless us?" (daily)
    C. "How much does He do it?" (lots -- He loads us)
    D. "What should be our response to God?" (gratefulness, thanksgiving)
VI. Memorize Philippians 4:19 and Psalm 68:19.
VII. Thank God for meeting our needs and loading us with blessings.

DAY 14

I. Memorize Philippians 4:19 and Psalm 68:19.
II. Read Matthew 6:9-13.
    A. "Which part of this prayer shows that God wants to meet our needs?" (v.11)
    B. "Notice that we are to pray for our present needs to be met -- not worry about the future."
III. Read Psalm 103:1-5.
List and discuss the blessings God desires to give to us.
IV. Thank God for His many blessings.

DAY 15

I. Review definition of contentment.
II. Memorize Philippians 4:19 and Psalm 68:19.

CONTENTMENT

DAY 15 (cont.)

III. "We have been studying Bible passages that talk about how God provides for our needs. When we have confidence that He will take care of us and do good things for us, we can be content more easily. Today we will be looking at more verses that promise God's goodness to us."
   A. Psalm 84:11 -- "We can be content with what we have because God gives us whatever is good for us, when we ask Him."
   B. Psalm 34:10
   C. Psalm 145:9 -- Emphasize "all."

IV. Ask God to help us have confidence that He will give us good things.

DAY 16

I. Memorize Philippians 4:19 and Psalm 68:19.
II. "Turn to Luke 3:14. John the Baptist is the one speaking in this verse. He is preaching to the people to repent and get ready for the coming of God's kingdom." (Read Luke 3:14.)
   A. "What did John have to say about contentment?" (Be content with your wages.)
   B. "Is it right to grumble and be dissatisfied?"
   C. "This doesn't mean a person shouldn't ask for a raise, or find a different job if he is not being paid fairly or enough to live on. But we shouldn't grump about our wages, and before looking for a different job, we should ask God what He wants us to do. He may show us we are the problem."
   D. Parents should give examples of times when God helped them to learn contentment with their earnings, or perhaps times they have failed in this area of their lives.
   E. "How could you apply this right now to your life?" (Perhaps a child needs to be content with the allowance he receives.)
III. Thank God for supplying our needs through Dad or Mom's job, and also for other ways He has supplied.

DAY 17

I. Memorize Philippians 4:19 and Psalm 68:19.
II. "Which of the Ten Commandments deals with being content? Read Exodus 20 to find out." (Exodus 20:17 gives the answer. Discuss.)
III. "What have you learned about contentment?" "How can you apply what you have learned to your life now?" "How can you apply these truths in the future?"

CONTENTMENT

DAY 17 (cont.)

IV. Review memorization
    A. I Timothy 6:6-11
    B. Philippians 4:11b
    C. Hebrews 13:5
    D. I John 2:15-17

V. Pray that God would make the truths we've learned about contentment live in us.

GRATITUDE

DAY 1

I. Introduction
   A. "What is gratitude?" (gratefulness, thankfulness)
   B. "Why is it important that we show gratitude to others?" (It is the appropriate response for kindness done to us, makes the giver feel good, does us good to be appreciative.)
   C. "To whom should we show gratitude?" (anyone who is kind to us, especially God)
   D. "Gratitude goes hand-in-hand with contentment. People who are content are usually grateful and appreciative. People who are unthankful (ungrateful) are usually also discontent."
   E. "What are some ways we can demonstrate gratitude?" (saying thank you, doing nice things in return)

II. Read Psalm 68:19.
   A. "Remember when we learned this verse during our contentment unit?"
   B. "Which part tells what good things God has given us?"
   C. "Which part is expressing gratefulness to God?"
   D. "Praising God is a way of showing gratitude to Him."

III. Read Psalm 103:1-5.
   A. "What good things are mentioned that God does for us?"
   B. "Which lines talk about being grateful for God's kindness?"
   C. "When we praise God for His goodness, we are being grateful to Him. God's heart is warmed and made happy when we appreciate Him verbally."

IV. Pray that we would cultivate grateful hearts. Thank God for His goodness. (Mention specific things for which we are thankful.)

DAY 2

I. "What are some reasons we decided it is important to be grateful?"
II. Read Psalm 100.
   A. List reasons we should be thankful to God:
      1. He made us.
      2. We belong to Him, so He cares for us like His sheep.
      3. He is good.
      4. His mercy is unlimited.
      5. His truth
   B. List how we are to show gratitude:
      1. Praise Him joyfully <u>out loud</u>. (v.1)
      2. Serve Him with gladness. (v.2)

GRATITUDE

DAY 2 (cont.)

        3. Sing to Him. (v.2)
        4. Thanksgiving (v.4)
        5. Praise (v.4)
        6. Bless His name (praise). (v.4)

III. Memorize Psalm 100.
IV. Have a special time of praising God. Use as many ideas from II. B. as possible.

DAY 3

I. Review yesterday's lesson.
II. Memorize Psalm 100.
III. "Let's talk about some other things God's Word says we should thank Him for."
    A. Read John 11:41.
        1. Discuss what is happening.
        2. Talk about being thankful that God hears and answers prayer.
    B. Read Romans 1:8 -- Thank God for brothers and sisters in Christ.
    C. Read I Corinthians 14:18 -- Thank God for prayer language.
    D. Read I Timothy 1:12.
        1. Thank God for helping us do His work.
        2. Thank Him for the privilege of doing His work in partnership with Him.
IV. Thank God for each of the things we have discussed today.

DAY 4

I. Memorize Psalm 100.
II. More things for which to thank God:
    A. Read Romans 6:17,18 and I Thessalonians 2:13.
        1. For those who are brought out of sin into His kingdom
        2. For those who receive the Word of God.
    B. Read I Timothy 4:3,4. (for food)
    C. Read I Thessalonians 5:18.
        1. Thank Him in all things.
        2. "Why can we do this with confidence?" (God is always good and loving.)
III. Thank God for these things.

GRATITUDE

DAY 5

I. Memorize Psalm 100.
II. "We talked last time about what to be thankful for. What were some things the Bible mentioned?"
    A. Answers to prayer (John 11:41)
    B. Christian brothers and sisters (Romans 1:8)
    C. Prayer language (I Cor. 14:18)
    D. Helping us serve Him and the privilege of serving Him (I Tim. 1:12)
    E. Those who get saved (Rom. 6:17,18 and I Thess. 2:13)
    F. Food (I Tim. 4:3,4)
    G. Our circumstances -- whatever they are (I Thess. 5:18)
    H. Forgiveness of sins (Psalm 103:3)
        Gratefulness for God's forgiveness -- Jesus' sacrifice on the cross -- should be the most important thing for which we are thankful.
    I. Healing (Psalm 103:3)
    J. Abundance of all blessings (Psalm 68:19)
    K. For making us (Psalm 100)
    L. His truth (Psalm 100)
III. Talk about other things for which we should be thankful, such as God's presence with us, His love and care, family, freedom in our country, God's protection and safe-keeping, etc.
IV. Have each child and parent choose two or three things for which to be thankful, from today's review, and spend time thanking God together for them.

DAY 6

I. Memorize Psalm 100.
II. "God actually commands His people to be thankful. In the Old Testament, the Israelites were to bring thank-offerings to Him. At that time, thank-offerings were animal sacrifices."
III. Read Colossians 3:15.
    A. "God inspires Paul to say, 'Be ye thankful.'"
    B. Memorize Colossians 3:15.
IV. Read Luke 6:35.
    A. "To whom is God kind?" (unthankful and evil)
    B. "How do you think God feels when we don't thank Him?" "How do you feel when people don't thank you?"
V. Pray for greater awareness to be thankful.

GRATITUDE

DAY 7

I. Memorize Psalm 100 and Colossians 3:15.
II. Read II Chronicles 32:24-26.
   A. "What had God done for Hezekiah?" (healed him -- The entire story is found in II Kings 20:1-11 and Isaiah 38:1-22.)
   B. "What is meant by, 'Hezekiah rendered not again according to the benefit done unto him'?" (He wasn't as thankful as he should have been.)
   C. "Why wasn't Hezekiah thankful?" (He was proud.)
   D. "What did God think about Hezekiah's unthankfulness?" (He was very angry.)
   E. "A proud heart is an unthankful heart. If we are not remembering to be grateful and thankful, we may have to repent of pride, as well as ingratitude."
   F. "What did Hezekiah do when he realized his sin of ingratitude and pride?" (He repented and humbled himself before God.)
   G. "What was God's response?" (He wasn't angry with Hezekiah anymore; judgment was averted.)
III. Pray for grateful, humble hearts. Pray for awareness of any unthankfulness in our lives, so we can repent.

DAY 8

I. Memorize Psalm 100 and Colossians 3:15.
II. Read Romans 1:18-25. (You may wish to reread in a modern translation, if using the King James, for greater understanding.)
   A. Discuss verse-by-verse.
      1. Verses 18,19 -- God is angered by the ungodliness and wickedness of men, because men know in their hearts what is right. God has put in every person a sense of there being a God. He has also given every person a conscience.
      2. Verse 20 -- Man has an innate understanding of God's existence. God's existence can be seen all around us -- even in the magnificence of the creation. Therefore, those who refuse to acknowledge God have no excuse for not knowing Him.
      3. Verse 21 -- Having this inner knowledge of God, some have refused to glorify Him as such, and have also refused to give Him the thanks He deserves. As a result of this ingratitude, they have developed their own ideas in their imaginations, as to what they want God to be like, and their hearts have become darkened to the truth about God.
      4. Verses 22,23 -- Expand on verse 21. Thinking they have become wiser, these people have really become fools, sometimes worshipping themselves, animals, and other idols.

GRATITUDE

DAY 8 (cont.)

        5. Verse 24 -- God has let them follow the foolish desires of their hearts, so that they now do unclean things and practice vile rituals as part of their warped religions.

        6. Verse 25 -- They have changed God's truth into twisted lies, and often worship God's creation, instead of Himself!

    B. "Who is without excuse?" (those who refuse to acknowledge God, those that don't know Him)

    C. "How did they get this way?" (v.21 -- by being unthankful, not glorifying God)

    D. "What was the result of their unthankfulness?" (v.21 -- became vain -- fruitless and proud -- in their thoughts, their hearts darkened; v.22 -- thought themselves wise, but were fools; v.23 -- had a corrupted idea of God -- heathenism, pantheism; v.24 -- became unclean, full of lust, perverted in lifestyle and worship)

    E. "This is how all pagan religions started. This is why so many are lost in sin today. It all started with unthankful, ungrateful hearts!"

III. Pray for true and sincere thankfulness toward God to be a way of life for us.

DAY 9

I. Memorize Psalm 100 and Colossians 3:15.

II. Review

    A. "What are some things we've talked about for which God wants us to thank Him?"

    B. "God is worthy to be thanked at all times."

    C. "What did we learn from Romans 1, yesterday?" (Review lesson.)

III. "For what should we be most thankful?"

    A. Talk about God's greatest gift to us -- Jesus.

    B. Talk about how we should never take Jesus' sacrifice for us for granted. We should always be thankful to Him for dying for us.

    C. "Did you know that when we deliberately sin and turn away from following God's plan for us that we are showing ingratitude to Jesus? We are being ungrateful that He died for us!"

IV. Thank Jesus for the great love for us which made Him give His life for us. Ask for forever-grateful hearts, which do not trample on His suffering.

V. The Lord's Supper shows thankfulness

    A. "There is a special thing we do together as believers that reminds us of Jesus' death and resurrection. Do you know what this celebration is?"

    B. "We call it the Lord's Supper, or Holy Communion. Some Christians prefer to call it Eucharist. Eucharist means gratitude."

GRATITUDE

DAY 9 (cont.)

    C. "When we celebrate Communion, we are not only remembering Jesus' death and resurrection -- we are giving our thanks and gratitude to Him for it. Communion is a thanksgiving celebration."

VI. Thank our Father for sending Jesus.

DAY 10

I. Memorize Psalm 100 and Colossians 3:15.
II. Read Matthew 7:12.
    A. "How does this verse tie in with gratitude?"
    B. "How do you feel when you do something nice for someone, and that person doesn't thank you?"
    C. "We must always be careful to thank others and show them we appreciate them. We need to be thankful, not only to God, but to other people."
    D. "What are some situations in which we could show thankfulness, and how would we go about expressing our appreciation?" (There are many ideas that could be discussed. One of the most obvious ways, yet one that is becoming increasingly rare, is thank you notes sent for gifts received. Thanking Sunday School teachers for their faithful teaching, thanks expressed when people take us with them, appreciation gifts -- especially small, home-made ones, even thanking Dad for taking the family out to lunch -- all these are ideas that could be used.)
III. Memorize Matthew 7:12.
IV. Pray for the sensitivity to thank and appreciate others.

DAY 11

I. Memorize Colossians 3:15 and Matthew 7:12.
II. Give the background to the following Scripture passage -- David and his household are fleeing Jerusalem because his son Absalom has taken the kingdom.
III. Read II Samuel 17:27-29.
    A. "What is happening?" (Some of David's loyal subjects are providing supplies for the fleeing royal family.)
    B. "Who is helping David?"
IV. Read II Samuel 19:31-40.
    A. "This part of the story takes place after Absalom has been killed, David's loyal army has defeated Absalom's army, and David is returning to Jerusalem to take over the kingdom again."
    B. "What had Barzillai done for David?" (He had been one of those who brought supplies to David's family, when they were running away from Absalom.)

GRATITUDE

DAY 11 (cont.)

        C. "What is David's response to Barzillai?" (He wants to reward and honor him.)

        D. "What is David showing by his actions toward Barzillai?" (gratitude)

V. Read I Kings 2:1-4,7.

        A. "Solomon is now reigning as king, and David is about to die. What does David instruct Solomon, concerning Barzillai's family?" (show them kindness and have them eat at the king's table)

        B. "What is David showing toward Barzillai?" (gratitude)

        C. "Keep in mind that this is many years after Barzillai had been kind to him. David continued in gratitude all of his life toward those who had shown him kindness. We should be like this also."

        D. "Never forget to have enduring gratitude toward those who have been good to you."

VI. Pray for hearts that will not forget past kindnesses. Pray for enduring gratitude.

DAY 12

I. Memorize Colossians 3:15 and Matthew 7:12.

II. If your children are knowledgeable in the Old Testament stories, you will be able to ask them the following questions. If not, the story background for today's lesson can be found in II Chronicles 22:10--24:14. You may want to tell them the story briefly. (This story was also discussed in the loyalty unit -- Day 10.)

        A. "Do you remember the story of King Joash?"

        B. "Was he a good king, or a bad king?" (good, for a long time, but he turned bad later in life)

        C. "Tell me the story of Joash."

III. Read II Chronicles 24:15-25.

        A. "How did Joash act, in comparison to David's treatment of Barzillai?"

        B. "Was Joash grateful to Jehoiada?" (no)

        C. "What had Jehoiada done for Joash?" (He had protected him from Athaliah, recaptured the throne for him, raised him as one of his own children, and guided him in knowing the Lord.)

        D. "Verse 22 tells us that Joash did not remember the kindness which Jehoiada had done to him. Does this mean that Joash couldn't recall what had happened? Did he just forget?" (no)

        E. "Joash was not absent-minded. Joash chose to forget what Jehoiada had done for him. Joash was not enduringly grateful, as David had been."

        F. "What was the result of Joash's ingratitude?"

           1. V.22 -- Zechariah called on God, as he was dying, to give justice to Joash.

           2. V.23,24 -- Syria came up against Judah to destroy it.

GRATITUDE

DAY 12 (cont.)

        3. V.25 -- Joash became filled with disease.
        4. V.25 -- Joash was killed by his own servants.
        5. V.25 -- Joash was not given honorable burial.
    G. "Judging from what happened to Joash as a result of his lack of appreciation, what do you think God thinks of ingratitude?"

IV. Discussion of gratitude unit
    A. "What have you learned from our gratitude unit?"
    B. "How will this affect your life?"
    C. "Have you seen any changes in your life already?" "What are they?"
    D. "Where do you see room for improvement?"

V. Thank God for teaching us about thankfulness and gratitude, through His Word. Pray for changed lives as a result of what we've learned.

TRUTHFULNESS

DAY 1

I. Introduction
   A. "Today we begin a new unit -- TRUTHFULNESS. What would be a good definition of truthfulness?"
   B. DEFINITION: "Truthfulness is saying, thinking, and living what is really so. The opposite of this would be saying, thinking, or living a lie."
   C. "Why is being truthful so important in God's eyes?" (God is truth; His Word is truth.)
   D. "God wants us to be like Him. That's why He teaches us about truthfulness in the Bible."

II. Read Psalm 19:7-10. Discuss each verse carefully, emphasizing the points listed below:
   A. V.7 -- Law of the Lord perfect (no mistakes, complete). His testimony is sure (unshakably true).
   B. V.8 -- His statutes right, His commandments pure (clean of error)
   C. V.9 -- His judgments true
   D. V.10 -- "Therefore, because of His truth, how can we feel about His Word?" (more desirable than wealth, sweet to us)

III. Read Psalm 119:140, 142, and 160.
   A. "Does God's Word have error or lies in it?" (v.140 -- very pure, v.142 -- is the truth)
   B. "Can we trust all of God's Word as truth, or is some of it just stories?" (v.160 -- true from the beginning)

IV. Thank God for the truth of His Word.

DAY 2

I. "What is our definition of truthfulness?" (Refer to Day 1.)
II. "Let's look at a few Scripture verses that tell us God's Word is completely true."
   A. Psalm 12:6 -- very pure, no imperfections
   B. Psalm 93:5 -- very sure, or certain
   C. II Samuel 7:28 -- "...thy words be true..."
   D. Proverbs 30:5 -- "<u>Every</u> word of God is pure..."
III. "Jesus also had some things to say about the truth of God's Word."
   A. John 10:35 -- "...the Scripture cannot be broken." (proved false, contradictory)
   B. John 17:17 -- God's Word is truth; we are sanctified (made clean and holy) by God's true Word.
IV. Thank God we can trust in the purity and truth of His Word.

TRUTHFULNESS

DAY 3

I. "Would God ever lie to us?" "How do we know He wouldn't lie?"
II. Read the following Scriptures and discuss:
   A. Titus 1:2
   B. Numbers 23:19
   C. Hebrews 6:18
III. "Because of these Scriptures we have just read, and the verses we studied in our last lesson, we can be confident God would never lie to us. It is not at all in His nature. He says exactly what He means."
IV. Thank God and tell Him how glad we are He cannot lie.

DAY 4

I. Review
   A. "What was our definition of truthfulness?"
   B. "What have we learned about God's truthfulness?"
   C. "What have we learned about the reliability of His Word?"
II. "Jesus says He is Himself truth." (Read the following verses together.)
   A. John 14:6 -- the way, truth, and life
   B. Revelation 3:7
   C. Revelation 3:14 – "Faithful and True" is one of the names, or titles, of Jesus.
   D. Revelation 19:11 -- again referring to Jesus as Faithful and True
III. "Proverbs 14:5 tells us, 'a faithful witness will not lie.' Since Jesus is the Faithful and True Witness, we know He will not lie. We can trust fully whatever He says."
IV. "If God is always truth, where do lies come from? Let's read John 8:44 to find out." (read)
   A. "The devil is the father of lies. He never, ever tells the truth. Even when he quoted Scripture to Jesus in the wilderness, he twisted it by pulling it out of context. He likes to tell half-truths. Half-truths are just another way of lying. They are not true at all. Can you explain a half-truth to me?"
   B. "This is why we must be so careful to know the whole Bible well, so we don't get fooled by the devil misquoting Scripture to us, in our minds, or through false teachers."
   C. "If the devil is the father of lies, does that mean we can blame it all on him when we lie?" (No, we must take responsibility for our own actions.)
V. Thank Jesus that He is the Faithful and True Witness. Ask Him to keep us from being fooled by the devil's lies.

TRUTHFULNESS

DAY 5

I. Review
   A. "Who is truth?"
   B. "Who cannot tell the truth?"
   C. "Who cannot lie?"
   D. "Whom do we want to be like?"

II. Read Proverbs 6:16-19.
   A. "What is an abomination?" (a hateful, grossly disgusting thing)
   B. "Notice that at least two of the seven things mentioned that God hates concern lying-- a lying tongue and a false witness that speaks lies. 'A heart that deviseth wicked imaginations' could also have to do with lying, because wicked imaginations are evil thoughts, which could be thoughts not filled with truth."

III. Read Proverbs 12:22.
   A. "What does God have to say about lying?" (an abomination)
   B. "What does God have to say about those that act in a true fashion?" (He delights in them.)

IV. "Today we have talked about three ways that a person can either tell the truth or lie:
   A. By speaking (Prov. 12:22, Prov. 6:17)
   B. In the thoughts (Prov. 6:18)
   C. In the actions (Prov. 12:22)"

V. Pray for grace to tell the truth in our thoughts, in our words, and in our actions.

DAY 6

I. Review
   A. "What was our definition of truthfulness?"
   B. "Do you remember what we learned yesterday about areas of our lives in which we need to be truthful?"
   C. "Truth must begin in our thoughts, and in our hearts. This involves our motives. We must tell the truth with our lips and also act in a truthful manner."

II. Read Leviticus 19:11.
   A. "To whom was God speaking?" (the Israelites of Moses' time)
   B. "Does this instruction apply to the Israelites of that time alone?" (no)
   C. "How do we know if it applies to Christians today?"
   D. "Let's see if there are further Scriptures concerning lying in the New Testament."

III. Read Colossians 3:9.
   A. "What is God saying?" (Do not lie to each other.)
   B. "To whom is He speaking?" (Christians)

TRUTHFULNESS

DAY 6 (cont.)

    C. "God very often repeats Old Testament commands in the New Testament. God's Word remains the same throughout the Old Testament and the New Testament when it relates to proper, loving behavior for people to follow. God's Word doesn't vary from generation to generation, people to people, except where He specifically says so, as in the case of Jewish sacrificial laws, which were done away with through Jesus' death."

IV. Read Ephesians 4:25.
    A. "What does it mean to put away lying?" (stop doing it)
    B. "What does 'we are members one of another' mean?" (Christians are all parts of the one body of Christ, the Church.)
    C. Memorize Ephesians 4:25.

V. Read Zechariah 8:16,17.
    A. "What does God want us to do?" (speak truth to others, execute judgment of truth -- act out truth, deal in fairness)
    B. "What does God hate?" (imagining evil against others, loving false oaths -- affirming something is so when it is not)

VI. "What would be a good way to summarize what we've read today?" (God says to be truthful -- don't lie.)

VII. Pray that God would give us determination to be truthful.

DAY 7

I. Memorize Ephesians 4:25.

II. Read Proverbs 14:5.
    A. "Explain a faithful witness to me."
    B. "Remember when we learned from Revelation that one of Jesus' names is Faithful and True? Jesus wants us to be faithful and true, as He is."

III. Read Proverbs 13:5.
    A. "How are we to feel about lying?" (We should hate it.)
    B. "Why should we hate lying?" (Lying is not of God's nature, but of the devil.)

IV. Read Psalm 119:163.
    A. "How is this verse similar to the one we just read?" (It again emphasizes that we must hate lying.)
    B. "What are we to love?" (God's Word, which is truth)
    C. "God's Word is truth. It is the opposite of lying."

V. Read Psalm 119:29-30a.
    A. "We are going to use this Scripture as our prayer today."
    B. Close by praying the Scripture passage. Have children add anything in their own words that they wish to say regarding truth.

TRUTHFULNESS

DAY 8

I. Memorize Ephesians 4:25.
II. "The Bible has so much to say about telling the truth. What are some of the things we have learned concerning truth and lying?"
III. Read Proverbs 12:17.
    A. "What does the person who speaks truth show to others?" (a righteous, holy life)
    B. "What does the liar show to others?" (deceit -- the opposite of holiness and righteousness)
IV. Read Proverbs 12:19.
    A. "What does God say about people who speak truth?" (They will live forever.)
    B. "What does He say about liars?" (Their lives are brief.)
V. Read Revelation 21:8.
    A. "What happens to liars at the end of time?" (They burn in the lake of fire.)
    B. "Lying is associated with all sorts of other evils. Notice what they are." (Reread verse and comment on some of the other sins mentioned.)
VI. Read Revelation 21:27.
    A. "Where can't liars enter?" (the heavenly city)
    B. "Why do you suppose they can't enter heaven?" (Heaven is a pure place, and nothing impure is allowed there. Lies are impure.)
VII. Read Revelation 22:15.
    A. "Who is left outside the heavenly city?" (among others, those who love lying)
    B. "Liars can't be with Jesus forever. Jesus hates lies. When we make a practice of lying, we separate ourselves from Jesus. Lying is a very serious sin. We don't have to be fearful, though, that if we ever told a lie, we won't go to heaven. If we ask Jesus to forgive us, He will, and we can go to heaven. But we must not make a practice of lying."
VIII. Read Psalm 120:2.
    A. Discuss briefly.
    B. Use as closing prayer.

DAY 9

I. Memorize Ephesians 4:25.
II. Read Ephesians 4:15.
    A. "How are we to speak the truth?" (in love)
    B. "What does this mean?"

TRUTHFULNESS

DAY 9 (cont.)

    C. "We must always choose our words carefully. There is a right way to say things and a wrong way, especially if we are speaking truth as a correction to someone." (Give examples.) "Our motive in speaking truth must always be love. We must be gentle. We don't have to blurt out things, just because they are true. We need to be wise about when to be silent. We need to ask God for help in speaking the right way."

    D. "What does this verse tell us will happen as we learn to speak the truth in love?" (We will grow, and the people we speak to will grow in Christ.)

III. Pray for discernment of when and how to speak truth, and when it is better to be silent.

DAY 10

I. Memorize Ephesians 4:25.
II. Read Proverbs 3:3,4.
    A. "Can you put each part of verse 3 in your own words?"
    B. "What does it mean to 'bind mercy and truth on our necks?'" (to have these qualities so evident in us that they are like lovely jewelry upon us)
    C. "What does it mean to 'write them on the table of our hearts?'" (speaks of our hearts as a writing tablet, or notebook. We must remember deep down inside to be merciful and truthful. Mercy and truth are to be heart attitudes.)
    D. "What promise is given us in verse 4, if we have mercy and truth from our hearts?" (We will find favor and good understanding -- or a good reputation -- with God and other people.)
    E. "If we have mercy and truth as an attitude in our hearts, it will show in our speech and actions."
III. Memorize Proverbs 3:3,4.
IV. Ask God to give us a heart attitude of truth and mercy.

DAY 11

I. Memorize and review Proverbs 3:3,4.
II. Read Matthew 12:33-37.
    A. "Tell me in your own words what Jesus was saying."
    B. "How would this relate to being truthful?"
    C. "Truthfulness, like any character trait, must start with an attitude of the heart. If we desire in our hearts to be truthful, and if we think true thoughts, our mouths will say truthful things."

TRUTHFULNESS

DAY 11 (cont.)

        D. "What does Jesus say about the words we speak, in verses 36 and 37?" (We will be held accountable for them, judged by them.)

        E. "How should this cause us to desire to be truthful?" (We don't want to grieve Jesus or be held accountable for telling lies.)

III.   Read Matthew 15:18,19.

"Here again we see the dangers of having wrong attitudes, such as lying, in our hearts. Wrong attitudes in the heart defile us (make us impure) and are bound eventually to leak out for everyone to see."

IV.   Pray for hearts that delight in truth.

DAY 12

I.   Memorize Proverbs 3:3,4.

II.   Review yesterday's lesson.

III.   Read Ephesians 6:14.

        A. "Here truth is mentioned as part of our spiritual armor. How do we go about being girded, or belted, with truth, and from where does this truth come?" (God's Word)

        B. "God's Word is truth, and we must read it and soak it in, if we would be girded with truth. Whenever we read the Bible, we should sincerely ask God to plant His Word deep in our hearts and memories. Then we will be filled with truth."

IV.   Read all of the section on spiritual armor and discuss, if desired. (found in Ephesians 6:10-18)

V.   Read Philippians 4:8.

"If we discipline our minds to think about the things this verse tells us to think about, we will have our hearts and our minds filled with truth."

VI.   Pray we would be girded with God's truth and that we would keep our hearts and minds filled with the truth of His Word.

DAY 13

I.   Memorize Proverbs 3:3,4.

II.   Review yesterday's lesson, especially Philippians 4:8.

III.   "We need to be truthful in our dealings with people and with God. God has much to say about being truthful toward Him. We'll be looking at a couple of Scriptures that talk specifically about this."

        A. Read Joshua 24:14.

            1. "What does God mean by serving Him in sincerity and truth?"

            2. "What might be ways a person wouldn't do this?"

TRUTHFULNESS

DAY 13 (cont.)

    B. Read Matthew 15:8,9.
        1. "Jesus is quoting Isaiah 29. He is telling the scribes and Pharisees they are not really serving God at all with their man-made rules."
        2. "Do you see any ways we could be guilty of honoring God with our lips, while our hearts are far from Him?"
        3. "What about if we sing praise songs, but we're letting our minds wander, instead of paying attention to the words and meaning them? What about if we say we believe the commandments in the Bible are right, but we don't obey them? Jesus said if we love Him, we'll obey His commandments."
        4. "If we only honor God with our lips, and not from our hearts, are we being truthful with God?"

IV. Pray for hearts truly sincere toward God.

DAY 14

I. Memorize Proverbs 3:3,4.
II. Read John 4:23,24.
    A. "How does God want to be worshipped?" (in spirit and truth)
    B. "What does this mean?"
    C. "Remember yesterday's lesson about serving God with lip-service while the heart is far from Him? This Scripture in John is talking about worshipping the way God wants to be worshipped -- from the heart."
III. "Let's look at some other verses that talk about being truthful in our hearts toward God."
    A. Read Psalm 15:1,2.
    "Who will live with God?" (the righteous person, who speaks truth in his heart)
    B. Read Psalm 51:6.
        1. "What does having 'truth in the inward parts' mean?" (truth in the heart)
        2. "Who wants this for us?" (God)
        3. "What has God promised?" (He will make us to know wisdom.)
        4. "God desires us to be truthful in our hearts, therefore He will help us to have that truth inside. He promises us His wisdom in our hearts. It is up to us whether we will accept God's wisdom (have truth) or reject God's wisdom (have lies inside)."
    C. Read Psalm 145:18.
        1. "What does God promise?" (to be near them that call upon Him)
        2. "What condition must we fulfill in order to receive this promise?" (call on Him in truth -- out of a sincere heart toward Him)

TRUTHFULNESS

DAY 14 (cont.)

IV. Pray for God's help in having a true and honest heart toward Him.

DAY 15

I. Review
   A. "What character trait have we been talking about, over the last few weeks?"
   B. "What was our definition of truthfulness?" (Refer to Day 1.)
   C. "Do you remember the three areas of our lives where we need to be truthful?" (what we say, thoughts/heart attitude, actions)
II. Read Romans 12:17.
   A. "What does this verse have to do with being truthful?"
   B. "Are we talking about truthfulness in the heart, speech, or actions?" (actions)
   C. "When we are honest in what we do, we are being truthful in our actions. When we are truthful in our actions, we are glorifying God and being good witnesses for Jesus."
   D. "Can you recall times you have acted in this way?"
III. Memorize Proverbs 3:3,4.
IV. Pray for grace to be honest, or truthful, in what we do.

DAY 16

I. Review/introduction
   A. "What kind of truthfulness were we learning about in our last lesson?" (truthfulness in actions)
   B. "What is another name for this?" (honesty)
   C. "Today we will look at another Bible passage concerning truthful actions."
II. Read I John 1:6,7.
   A. "What does it mean to 'walk in darkness?'" (live contrary to God's ways)
   B. "What does the Bible say we are doing if we live this way?" (lying, not <u>doing</u> the truth)
   C. "What would be the opposite of acting this way?" (doing truth, which is walking in the light)
   D. "When we do truth (walk in the light), we can live without fearfulness, because we have nothing to hide. Liars are always fearful, hiding their secrets from others, hoping no one finds out the truth about them. What a blessing to be free from that fear! We can be free of fear if we live honest lives before God and man."

TRUTHFULNESS

DAY 16 (cont.)

      E. "What blessing is mentioned concerning those who 'walk in the light?'" (fellowship -- good relationship -- with other people, with God; cleansing from sin)
III. Memorize Proverbs 3:3,4.
IV. Pray that God would free us from walking in darkness and the fear it brings. Pray for grace to walk in the light.

DAY 17

I. Memorize Proverbs 3:3,4.
II. "Remember what we discussed in our last lesson?" (Review walking in darkness/walking in light concepts.)
III. Read I John 2:4-6.
      A. "Who is a liar?" (the person who says he knows God, but doesn't keep God's commandments)
      B. "'The truth is not in him,' the Bible says."
      C. "Verse 6 tells us how to be truthful in our actions. What does it say to do?" (live as Jesus lived)
      D. "If we ask ourselves, 'What would Jesus do?' and then act accordingly, we will find ourselves 'walking in the light,' living truthful lives, honest in our deeds."
IV. Pray that we could live honest lives, keeping God's commandments, living as Jesus would.

DAY 18

I. Memorize Proverbs 3:3,4.
II. Read I John 3:18.
      A. "Can you put this verse in your own words?"
      B. "Is this verse saying we shouldn't be loving in the way we speak to others?"
      C. "It is saying our actions speak louder than our words. If we say we love someone, but then don't act in a loving way, we are lying. Our words, if they are truthful ones, will be backed up by corresponding truthful actions."
III. Read Exodus 18:21.
      A. Give background story. Moses had become overwhelmed with too many responsibilities in caring for the needs of the Israelite people. At the suggestion of his father-in-law, and with God's approval, judges were chosen from among the people to help him with these duties.
      B. "What kind of people are useful to God?" (men who fear God, <u>men of truth</u>)
      C. "If we expect to be used of God, we must be people of truth."

TRUTHFULNESS

DAY 18 (cont.)

IV. Pray that we would be truthful in our actions, and be useful to God.

DAY 19

I. Memorize Ephesians 4:25 and Proverbs 3:3,4.
II. Read John 8:31,32.
    A. "How do we go about knowing the truth?" (continue in God's Word)
    B. "What will happen when we know the truth?" (We will be made free.)
    C. "Free from what?" (fear -- refer to walking in light lesson -- Day 16, free from bondage to sin and the devil, free from eternal death. There is a freeing power in the Gospel.)
    D. "We must continue in God's Word -- read and meditate on it -- if we want to be filled with truth. Do you remember when we discussed the importance of knowing God's Word thoroughly from Genesis to Revelation? Why did we say this was important?" (so we won't be deceived by false teachers, so we can live like God would want us to)
III. "Let's see how much you can remember of what we have learned in our truthfulness unit." (Discussion should follow.)
IV. Pray that we would know the truth and be made free by it. Thank God for teaching us about truthfulness. Ask Him to make this knowledge bear fruit in our lives.

SERVANTHOOD

DAY 1

I. Introduction
   A. "Over the next few weeks, we'll be talking about being a servant to others. Can you think of any people in the Bible who were servants in the way they acted toward others?" (Jesus, Joseph, Abraham, Samuel)
   B. "Can you think of people you know who have a servant attitude toward others?" (People such as parents, particular Christians at the local church, etc. may be suggested.)
   C. "Let's define what it means to have a servant heart. How would a person having a godly servant attitude behave?"
      1. Notice what needs to be done and do it without waiting to be asked (initiative)
      2. Cheerfully do what is asked
      3. Unselfishly give of time, self (generosity)
   D. "As the days go on, we'll be reading what God says about servanthood, seeing how Bible characters acted this way, and practicing being servants ourselves."

II. "Lord, teach us to be servants. Open our eyes to opportunities you give us to serve, and help us to cheerfully do it."

DAY 2

I. Review
   A. "What are we studying in Character Building?" (servanthood, service)
   B. "What does it mean to be a servant?"
   C. "Who was the greatest servant of all?" (Jesus)

II. "We can learn so much about servanthood from what Jesus taught, and from the way He lived. We'll be examining closely what Jesus said and did, so that we can become better servants."

III. Read John 13:1-17.
   A. Verse 1 -- "Notice that this verse says what Jesus did -- washing the disciples' feet, serving them -- was loving them. When we serve others we are showing love to them."
   B. Verse 3 -- "This verse tells us Jesus acted as a servant, knowing full well that He was God and had all authority. He did not think it was beneath the King of Kings to serve!"
   C. "Do you think what Jesus did for His disciples was pleasant work?" (very humbling)

SERVANTHOOD

DAY 2 (cont.)

- D. Verse 14 -- "Was Jesus telling the disciples we should have foot-washing ceremonies?" (no) "What principle was He teaching?" (Esteem others better than ourselves -- deference; serve one another with joy.)
- E. "Jesus says in verse 16 that if He Who is greatest of all acted as a servant, we who are His followers must do likewise."
- F. "What promise does Jesus give in verse 17?" (If we serve, as Jesus did, we will be happy.)
- G. "Those who serve cheerfully are happy people."

IV. "Lord, help us to be as You were -- cheerfully serving others."

DAY 3

I. "What were some things we said describe a servant?" (Refer to Day 1.)
II. "How did Jesus live out servanthood?"
- A. He healed others.
- B. He provided food. (fed 5,000 and 4,000)
- C. Washed disciples' feet
- D. Taught them
- E. Blessed the children -- had time for others

III. Read Philippians 2:3-15.
- A. Verse 3 -- "If we have a servant's heart, what attitude are we to have?" (not to cause strife or to be seeking glory for ourselves, be humble, think of others as better than ourselves)
- B. "What does verse 4 have to say about servanthood?" (We should be concerned about the needs of others.)
- C. Verse 5 -- "What does this mean, 'Let this mind be in you, which was also in Christ Jesus . . .?'" (Jesus was a servant -- He was concerned about the needs of others, as in verse 4. We are to be like Him.)
- D. Verses 6-8 -- "Just as we talked about in our last lesson, Jesus was fully aware that He was God of the whole universe, yet He deliberately chose to humble Himself and be a servant."
- E. Verse 9 -- "God the Father blessed and honored Jesus because He humbled Himself and became a servant."
- F. Verse 14 -- "How are we to do our service?" (without murmuring and arguing)
- G. Verse 15 -- "Why are we to serve cheerfully, without complaining?" (so we will be blameless, so we can shine for Jesus as good witnesses to the world)

IV. Memorize Philippians 2:3-15.
V. "Lord Jesus, help us to be humble servants, as You were. Help us to serve cheerfully, without arguing or complaining."

SERVANTHOOD

DAY 4

I. Memorize Philippians 2:3-15.
II. Application of what we have learned of service
    A. "Have you been asking God in your personal prayer time to help you be a servant?"
    B. "Have you been more aware of ways you can serve?"
    C. "Try to keep your eyes open for ways you can help out, without waiting to be asked. Pitch in and do things voluntarily. Even if no one else notices, God will, and He will be pleased."
    D. "Right now, I want you to look around you and spend fifteen minutes serving by doing what you see needs doing. When we do what needs to be done without waiting to be asked, this is called <u>initiative</u>." (Proceed to some hands-on learning about serving. Younger children may need some hints to help them get started.)
III. Thank God for showing us a practical way to serve.

DAY 5

I. Review
    A. "What is initiative?" (doing what needs to be done without waiting to be asked)
    B. "How did you show initiative yesterday?" (Remind, if necessary, of the service-in-action lesson of the previous day.)
    C. "How have you shown initiative today -- or how do you plan to show it?"
II. Read Matthew 10:40-42.
    A. "What point is Jesus trying to make?" (Whatever we do with love of Jesus as our motive will be rewarded.)
    B. "Do we have to always be doing things other people see as important in order to be serving God?" (no)
    C. "Do people think giving a cold drink to a little child is important?" (No, generally people tend to think little children are not as important as grown-ups.)
    D. "What does God think about it?" (God thinks little people are just as important as big people, so service to them is very valuable in His sight.)
III. Discuss any incidents you may know of people being involved in service in small ways -- especially in helping children. (I told my daughter about a woman who made a point of using great tenderness and patience when helping her small children to dress. She said she always tried to imagine she was doing it for the Christ Child.)
IV. Memorize Matthew 10:42. Also memorize Philippians 2:3-15.
V. Pray to be faithful to serve in small ways.

SERVANTHOOD

DAY 6

I. Review
  - A. Memorize and discuss Matthew 10:42.
  - B. "Whom does God see as being important?" "Whom does He want us to serve?" (God sees all people as being important -- even those we consider insignificant. He wants us to have a serving love toward the most lowly.)

II. Read Mark 9:33-37.
  - A. "About what were the disciples fighting?" (which one would be greatest in Jesus' kingdom)
  - B. "What do you think Jesus meant by, 'If any man desire to be first, the same shall be last of all, and servant of all?'"
  - C. "Do you think children were considered important in Jesus' day?" (no)
  - D. "Did Jesus think children were important?" "How do you know?"
  - E. "When we serve people not generally considered important, whom are we really serving?" (Jesus, God the Father)

III. Memorize Philippians 2:3-15.

IV. Pray for help in seeing the needs of others and meeting them.

DAY 7

I. Memorize Matthew 10:42 and Philippians 2:3-15.

II. Read Mark 10:35-45.
  - A. "Why were the other disciples angry with James and John?" (They also wanted to be the greatest.)
  - B. "What did Jesus say about those who are great in God's kingdom?" (must minister to, or serve, others)
  - C. "Whom would they serve?" (v.44 -- all)
  - D. "How does the world think of greatness?" (Those who rule over others are great.)
  - E. "Is this the same as, or opposite of, what God says about greatness?" (opposite)
  - F. "Most of the time the world's view of things and God's view are totally opposite of each other."
  - G. "What does Jesus say about Himself in verse 45?" (He came to serve, not to be served.)

III. Pray that we could learn to serve as Jesus did.

DAY 8

I. Memorize Matthew 10:42 and Philippians 2:3-15.

II. Read Luke 22:24-27.
  - A. "What is a benefactor?" (someone who does good to another person)

SERVANTHOOD

DAY 8 (cont.)

    B. "What did Jesus say a great person would be like?" (a younger person, a servant)
    C. "Younger people were not considered as important as their elders, so Jesus was indicating they should serve and show respect as younger people would to older people."
    D. "Is the one serving, or the one being served, normally thought of as the greater?" (the one being served)
    E. "Which did Jesus say He was like?" (the one who serves)

III. Pray that we would serve others cheerfully.

DAY 9

I. Memorize Matthew 10:42 and Philippians 2:3-15.
II. Review
    A. "What do we call it when we go ahead and do things we see need to be done, without being asked?" (initiative)
    B. "How have you shown initiative over the past week?"
    C. "Have you been praying that God would help you grow in having initiative?"
III. Service-in-action
"Find all the things you can do to help around our home, and work on some of them over the next fifteen minutes." (Helpful suggestions or hints can be given to smaller children. After working, discuss what was done by each.)
IV. Thank God for what He is teaching us about service.

DAY 10

I. Memorize Matthew 10:42 and Philippians 2:3-15.
II. Read Matthew 25:31-46.
    A. "What have you learned about service in this Scripture passage? Tell me in your own words what Jesus is saying."
    B. "List the ways of serving mentioned."
        1. Feeding the hungry
        2. Refreshing the thirsty
        3. Sheltering (lodging) those that need a place
        4. Clothing the naked
        5. Visiting the sick and imprisoned
    C. "How could we live out these ways of serving in our time?"
    D. "Whom are we really serving when we serve others?" (Jesus)
    E. "We should keep in mind Whom we are really serving -- or not serving. It would help us to do these things more cheerfully."

SERVANTHOOD

DAY 10 (cont.)

      F. "What happened to those who did these things?" "To those who did not?"

      G. "The normal Christian life should have service flowing from it quite naturally."

III. Plan a family project based on the ways of serving listed in Matthew 25:31-46. Some possibilities might be collecting clothes for a community clothes closet, taking groceries to an unemployed family, visiting a sick person from the neighborhood or church, sponsoring a needy child in another country and having the children contribute to the sponsorship with allowance money or money earned through odd jobs.

IV. Pray for eyes to see how to serve and hearts willing to do it.

DAY 11

I. Memorize Matthew 10:42 and Philippians 2:3-15.

II. Read Luke 17:7-10.

      A. "What lesson is Jesus teaching us about servanthood in this passage?"

      B. "When we serve the Lord or other people, we shouldn't be expecting praise for our actions. We shouldn't be thinking, 'Hey, I'm a really great person for serving God so well.' We should realize we are simply doing what God expects of us. Does this mean God doesn't appreciate us when we do well?" (No, He does, but this deals with our attitudes.)

III. Read Matthew 6:1-6, 16-18.

      A. "How are these verses connected with the verses we just read in Luke?" (They talk of various kinds of service, our attitude, and God's response to our service.)

      B. "What did Jesus not want us to do?" (make a show of our service to others)

      C. "What does Jesus want of us?" (to do our service quietly, modestly, without show)

      D. "Does God honor and appreciate our service?" (yes) "How do you know?" (verses 4, 6, and 18)

IV. Pray we would do our service modestly and quietly, not becoming proud about it.

DAY 12

I. Memorize Matthew 10:42 and Philippians 2:3-15.

II. Review and introduction to new material

      A. "What did we talk about yesterday?" (Review the main ideas of lesson.)

      B. "Is it easy to be a servant?" (no) "Many times it isn't easy. Let's look at what Jesus taught about this."

SERVANTHOOD

DAY 12 (cont.)

III. Read Luke 9:23-25.
  A. "What did Jesus say we must do if we are planning to follow Him?" (deny ourselves, take up our cross daily)
  B. "Jesus is using a word picture, when He says to take up our cross daily. What is a word picture?" (words creating an idea that we can picture in our minds.)
  C. "What idea is He trying to give us when He speaks of taking the cross daily?" (daily dying to -- or putting aside -- our own desires, to give preference to what God wants of us; also to give preference to meeting the needs of others)

IV. Read John 12:24-26.
  A. "Is Jesus really speaking of wheat seeds?" (no) "What is He talking about?" (dying to self -- our own desires)
  B. "What did Jesus say will happen if we die to our desires?" (Our lives will bear fruit, we'll have eternal life, we will be always with Jesus, and the Father will honor us.)
  C. "Does this mean serving -- doing good works -- will give us eternal life?" (No, our service is always to be done because we love Jesus. It naturally flows from our love for Him.)

V. "Dear Jesus, please help us to die to our own desires so we can serve You and others. Thank You that You have promised to have us always be with You, if we are your servants."

DAY 13

I. Memorize Matthew 10:42 and Philippians 2:3-15.
II. Review the previous lesson.
III. Read James 4:17.
  A. "Can you put this verse in your own words?"
  B. "How can we apply this to our lives?"
  C. "How do you think God feels when we don't help someone who needs us?" (sad, disappointed)
IV. Read I John 3:17,18.
  A. "What does God want us to do?" (share our things with those in need)
  B. "If we don't do this, what does God say about us?" (We don't have the love of God in us.)
  C. "How are we to show that we are loving?" (v.18 -- in our deeds)
V. "Dear Lord, help us to be eager to help others and meet their needs."

SERVANTHOOD

DAY 14

I. Memorize Matthew 10:42 and Philippians 2:3-15.
II. "Today we will be learning about a particular person in the Bible who is mentioned because she had a servant's heart. Turn to Romans 16:1,2." (read)
    A. "Who was the lady who was a servant?" (Phoebe)
    B. "Whom did she serve?" (church at Cenchrea)
    C. "Phoebe was known as a servant in her local church. She had a reputation even beyond her church for her service."
    D. "What kind of service did Phoebe do that is specifically mentioned?" (She had succored -- comforted, refreshed, encouraged -- many, including Paul.)
    E. "Phoebe probably had been the type of person who encouraged the discouraged brothers and sisters. Very likely she was hospitable -- welcoming people into her home. She was a person who could see the needs of others, and do something to meet those needs."
    F. "Very likely Phoebe is the one carrying this letter to the Romans from Paul, or is at least in the messenger's group. She evidently is traveling to Rome to do some work for the Lord, because Paul calls on the Roman church to receive (welcome) her and assist her."
    G. "How can we be servants in our own local church, as Phoebe was?" (Discussion should follow.)
III. "Lord, please teach us to serve our brothers and sisters as Phoebe did. Give us specific ideas how to do this, and help us to act on your promptings."

DAY 15

I. Memorize Matthew 10:42 and Philippians 2:3-15.
II. Read I Corinthians 9:19-23.
    A. "What, in your own words, is Paul saying?"
    B. "In verse 19, Paul says he was not born a slave, but had chosen to be a servant -- to whom?" (all) "For what purpose?" (to gain more)
    C. "What is Paul seeking to gain more of?" (souls for Jesus)
    D. "Paul chose to be a servant to all, subjecting himself to each person's life circumstances, understanding and fitting into each person's background, in order to win that one to Christ." (verses 20-23)
    E. "When we have a servant's attitude toward others, it softens their hearts, so that we can win them to Christ."
III. Pray that we could willingly serve others, so that they would give their lives to Jesus.

SERVANTHOOD

DAY 16

Note: Today's lesson is directed toward girls and young women. Tomorrow's lesson will be directed toward boys and young men. You may either choose to use both lessons, or use the one that pertains to the particular make-up of your family. Mothers may wish to do one lesson with their daughters, while fathers study the alternate lesson with their sons.

I. "Today we are going to look at how a woman should serve in her own home. Let's turn to Titus 2:3-5." (read)
   A. "What were the old women to teach the young women?" (to be sober -- serious-minded and wise; love their husbands and children; be discreet -- prudent or careful in actions and words; chaste -- pure and modest; obedient to husbands)
   B. "Why is it important for homemakers who love Jesus to act this way?" (so God's Word isn't ridiculed)
   C. "What might it mean to be 'keepers at home?'" (taking care of children, keeping house clean, providing good meals and clothing, a warm and loving home for family)
   D. "How is this being a servant?"
   E. "What might be the opposite of this godly behavior?" (seeking own pleasure instead of taking care of family's needs, running around the neighborhood to chatter and gossip)
   F. "Do you think this is an easy calling -- to be a godly homemaker?" (no)
   G. "How might dying to self be involved in being a godly homemaker?"

II. Pray that God would teach us how to be the kind of homemakers He wants us to be.

DAY 17

Note: This is a lesson directed to boys and young men.

I. Read Ephesians 5:25-32 and Ephesians 6:4.
   A. "You may not think this section of Scripture applies to you, but it is important to know what God says to men now, so that you can use this knowledge when you do become a husband and father. Hide God's Word away in your hearts, and God will remind you of it later on when you need it."
   B. "In what attitude are husbands to love their wives?" (as Christ loved the Church)
   C. "To what lengths did Christ go to serve and love the Church?" (to the point of death; He gave His all)
   D. "How are men to love their wives, according to verse 28?" (as they love themselves)

SERVANTHOOD

DAY 17 (cont.)

  E. "What might be some reasons for saying he is loving himself, if he does this?" (When a man and woman marry, they become one. Also, the man who loves his wife in this way will find life in his home to be much more peaceful, since the wife will feel secure, and can respond to her family with love more easily.)

  F. "How will a husband's love and service to his wife glorify God?" (It shows the world a true picture of Christ's love for the Church.)

  G. "How is the father in Ephesians 6:4 serving his children?" (being kind to them, bringing them up to know the Lord and to follow His ways)

  H. "Do you think this is an easy task for fathers?" (It takes great diligence and much prayer to find God's wisdom for raising each child in the right way.)

II. Pray that God would help us to remember these truths when they are needed in times to come. Pray that He would begin to work a servant's heart in each one of us even now. Pray for Dad to have these qualities in our home at this time.

DAY 18

Note: This lesson is also directed mainly toward girls and young women, but could be used to instruct young men in what to watch for when looking for a wife in future years. Use your own discretion, depending on the make-up of your family, as to whether the lesson should be used with the entire family, or used simply with the daughters. Age of the children may also be a deciding factor as to its usefulness.

I. Read Proverbs 31:10-31.

  A. "See if you can list the ways mentioned that the virtuous (good and godly) woman serves her family." (does good to husband, makes clothes, gathers food, feeds family, plants garden, works hard for family, works into night and rises early to do her chores, helps needy, provides some of family's income by selling clothes she makes, buys wisely (good steward), speaks wisdom and kindness, watches over household well, isn't idle)

  B. "She sounds like an impossibly perfect person, doesn't she? God is giving us a general idea of some of the kinds of things in which a godly woman might be involved. He is not saying that if you don't do all these things you are not a virtuous woman. He is showing us some wonderful character qualities and attitudes that she has, such as being industrious, caring for the needs of others, being trustworthy, and being kind."

  C. "What is her reward?" (verses 11, 28-30, 31 -- husband trusts her, husband and children praise her, blessed with the fruit of her hands -- prosperity increases, reputation to be praised throughout town)

II. Pray for Mom to grow in these attributes of a good housewife. Also that children would store away these truths in their hearts for future use.

SERVANTHOOD

DAY 19

I. "Over the next few days we will be learning about service in the workplace. This will be important information to tuck away in your minds and hearts for the future, but you can also apply it now in doing your chores around the home."

II. Read Colossians 3:22-25.
   A. "We have studied this Scripture passage before. Do you remember it?"
   B. "What does God say about how a servant should act -- about the servant attitude?"
      1. "Obey in all things" -- of course does not include obeying if one is commanded to do something sinful.
      2. "Not with eye service, as men-pleasers" -- "We don't just try to look like we're working hard when someone is watching. We should always do our best, whether we're being watched or not."
      3. "Do your work in singleness of heart. Do it with all your might, because you are really serving God." (verses 22,23)
      4. "Keep in mind that God is watching. You will either be rewarded, or not rewarded, according to how you serve. You can't get away with sloppy work. God sees it." (verses 24,25)

III. Pray for God's help to serve with the whole heart, as unto Him.

DAY 20

I. Read Ephesians 6:5-8.
   A. "This Scripture is very similar to the one in Colossians we studied yesterday."
   B. "What might it mean, that servants should serve their masters with fear and trembling?" (v.5 -- We should serve our employers -- or parents -- with respectful, honoring attitudes.)
   C. "Again we are reminded not only to serve when we're being watched by the employer or parent, but to serve from the heart. This is doing the will of God." (v.6)
   D. "What do you suppose verse 7 means, 'with good will doing service?'" (serving cheerfully)
   E. "What does God promise to those that serve from the heart, and cheerfully?" (v.8 -- They will receive blessing, reward from God.)
   F. "How do you think you can apply these lessons about service in the workplace to your own life right now?"

II. "Dear Father, help us remember it is really You we are serving. Help us to serve cheerfully from our hearts, remembering that You are always watching."

SERVANTHOOD

DAY 21

I. Read I Timothy 6:1,2.
    A. "How are we to treat our employers (or parents)?" (with respect, honor)
    B. "Why?" (so God and His teachings won't be blasphemed, or made fun of)
    C. "Do you think how we serve on the job, or around home, affects our witness for Jesus?"
    D. "How are Christians to serve Christian employers?" (Especially honor them, and don't despise them, because they are brothers in the Lord.)
    E. "Sometimes Christians may think they can take advantage of their employers because the boss is also a Christian. They might think they should be able to get away with more. God says this is not a right attitude."

II. Ask God to put these truths in our hearts and help us to remember them and apply them to our lives.

DAY 22

I. Begin review - memorizing Philippians 2:3-15.
II. Read I Peter 2:18-23.
    A. "To whom should employees be subject?" (their bosses)
    B. "What does it mean to be subject to someone?" (to give in to his will, his authority)
    C. "In what attitude are employees to be subject to their bosses?" (with all fear)
    D. "'With all fear' doesn't mean to be afraid of your boss. It means to show respect."
    E. "What kind of bosses are to be obeyed and respected?" (both the good, kind ones and the bad, mean ones)
    F. "Why should even mean bosses be obeyed and respected?"
        1. God says so. (v.18)
        2. If a person suffers for doing right, God will reward him. (v.19)
    G. "Read verses 19-23 again."
    H. "Sometimes you will be blamed when you didn't do anything wrong. Sometimes you might get into trouble for doing what is right in God's eyes. You never have to obey an employer if he tells you to do something wrong. Perhaps your employer will expect you to help him to be dishonest. Though you should not obey when told to do something wrong, you do need to be respectful in explaining why you can't in good conscience do what is being asked. If you are blamed for something, you must never answer back rudely. Perhaps you will even be punished unfairly, but God will reward you for suffering patiently. He will make it right in the end. Jesus suffered unjust treatment. He would want us to respond in the same way He did."

SERVANTHOOD

DAY 22 (cont.)

    I.   "Do you think any of this lesson could apply to how things are handled in our home?" "How?"

III.   "Lord, thank You for teaching us how to act toward employers. Please put this information deep in our hearts so we can use it both now and later in life."

DAY 23

I.   Review / memorization of Philippians 2:3-15.

II.   Read Titus 3:1 and 8.
    A.   "What are we to be ready for and to be careful to do?" (good works)
    B.   "Doing good works means serving. God wants us to be always ready to do good and to be careful to maintain, or keep on doing, good works. We are called to serve others, if we are Christians."

III.   Read Matthew 6:24.
    A.   "Is it possible to serve God and others at the same time?" (Yes, when we serve others, we are also doing it for Jesus.)
    B.   "But this verse says we can't serve two masters. What does it mean?" (It is saying we can't serve God and money at the same time.)
    C.   "We can't be working for Jesus single-heartedly and also working for personal gain or selfish pleasure. This is also part of dying to self."

IV.   "Lord, help us to be careful to keep on serving. Help us also remember to serve You alone -- not our selfish, greedy desires."

HOSPITALITY

DAY 1

I. Introduction
   A. "What is HOSPITALITY?"
   B. DEFINITION: Making others welcome in our home.
   C. "We're going to see what God wants to teach us about hospitality in the Bible."
II. Read Genesis 18:1-8.
   A. "Who is showing hospitality?" (Abraham)
   B. "To whom is he showing hospitality?" (three men)
   C. "Who were these three men?" (God and two angels in human form)
   D. "List the ways Abraham showed hospitality to them."
      1. Ran to meet them
      2. Bowed to show respect
      3. Invited them to his home
      4. Washed their feet
      5. Invited them to rest under a shade tree
      6. Fed them a nice meal
   E. "Do you think Abraham realized the identity of his guests right away?" (He probably didn't. He would have done the same for anyone.)
III. Pray that God would help us learn to be more hospitable.

DAY 2

I. Introduction
   A. "What did we begin to learn about in our last lesson?" (hospitality)
   B. "What is hospitality?"
   C. "Hospitality is a special type of service. Someone who is hospitable is showing he is a servant. We get our word hospital from this word. People who work in hospitals are serving others by caring for their needs while they are sick."
   D. "Who showed hospitality in our last lesson?"
   E. "How did Abraham show hospitality?" (review)
II. Read Luke 7:36-50.
   A. "Did Simon the Pharisee act hospitably toward Jesus?" (no)
   B. "What things did Simon neglect to do for Jesus?" (didn't wash His feet or even give Him water to do it Himself, no welcoming kiss -- like our handshake, no anointing oil)
   C. "The things Simon didn't bother to do for Jesus were common courtesies which should have been shown to any guest. Simon was extremely rude to Jesus in not doing these things."

HOSPITALITY

DAY 2 (cont.)

      D. "What do you think this lesson from the Bible could teach us?" (We should be very careful to treat our guests with courtesy and thoughtfulness.)

III. Pray God to instill in us a thoughtfulness and courtesy toward other people -- especially those we have in our home as guests.

DAY 3

I. Read Romans 12:9-13.
    A. "This section of Scripture gives us some guidelines for good ways for Christians to act toward other people. Loving without dissimulation means we aren't just to pretend to love -- we are to love sincerely. We are to be kind and affectionate, and prefer others in honor before ourselves, which is deference."
    B. "Do you remember our unit on deference? In it we talked about being a gracious host or hostess. This is all part of being hospitable and having a servant's heart." (Discuss what is involved in being a gracious host or hostess.)
    C. "What does Paul specifically mention in verse 13, that we are to do?" (be given, or prone, to hospitality)

II. Other Scriptures to be read and discussed:
    A. I Timothy 3:2 and Titus 1:8 -- Bishops (church leaders) are required to be proven in their hospitality.
    B. Hebrews 13:1,2 -- Relate to Abraham's entertaining of God and angels.
    C. III John 5-8 -- Encouragement to be hospitable
    D. III John 9,10 -- Example of church leader who was not given to hospitality, nor would he allow others to be

III. Pray that we would be given to hospitality, that we would grow in this way of serving.

DAY 4

I. Review
    A. "What does hospitality mean?"
    B. "What are some good and bad examples of hospitality that we have studied?" (Recall Abraham and Simon the Pharisee. Contrast their behaviors.)
    C. Review yesterday's Scriptures briefly.

II. Read I Peter 4:8,9.
    A. "What is 'fervent charity?'" (heartfelt love)
    B. "What does fervent charity, or heartfelt love, have to do with hospitality?" (It is the attitude we should have toward our guests.)

HOSPITALITY

DAY 4 (cont.)

- C. "What do you think Peter means by, 'Use hospitality one to another without grudging?'" (We should do it cheerfully, not having a stingy heart.)
- D. "When you welcome someone into your home, you should do it with a heart of being truly glad to have that person with you. Make him feel at home. Offer refreshments. If your guests have come for dinner, fix a really nice meal, if possible. Share freely what you have."

III. "Lord, please teach us to be loving and gracious to our guests. Help us to give of our very best to them, just as we would to You."

DAY 5

I. Read Luke 14:7-14.
- A. "In this section, Jesus is giving instructions for how both guests and hosts should act. Let's look at verses 12-14 in particular."
- B. "What type of hospitality is Jesus suggesting?" (to the poor and handicapped, those who cannot repay)
- C. "How could we act this out in our lives?" (discuss)
- D. "What other ways could we show hospitality?" (Invite people for meals who are friends, newcomers at church, visiting relatives, new neighbors, needy, missionaries. Invite for an evening. Make home open to children whose parents are not home when they get out of school. Babysitting for needy neighbors without charge when they really need a helping hand.)
- E. "Some other ways families have shown hospitality are by giving missionaries or traveling gospel groups a place to stay, loaning them their cars, giving unwed mothers a place to live. We may not be able to do all of these, but we should do what we can. Our family needs to cultivate hospitality."

II. Plan a hospitality project and carry it through.

III. Review what has been learned personally by each member of the family about hospitality.

IV. "Lord, help us to grow in hospitality in our family."

Made in the USA
Middletown, DE
17 May 2022